Werr 7/13
THOR 9/17

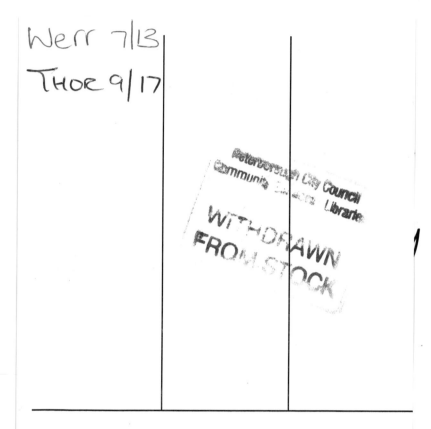

PETERBOROUGH LIBRARIES

24 Hour renewal line 08458 505606

This book is to be returned on or before the latest date shown above, but may be renewed up to three times if the book is not in demand. Ask at your local library for details.

Please note that charges are made on overdue books

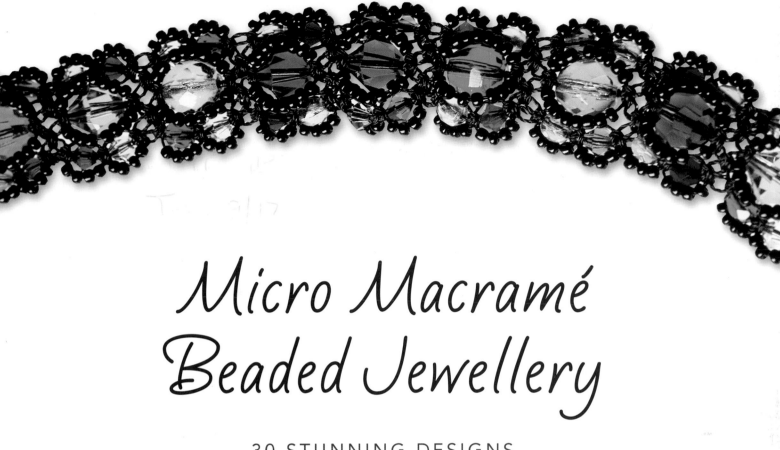

Micro Macramé
Beaded Jewellery

30 STUNNING DESIGNS
USING CRYSTALS AND CORDS

Annika deGroot

Search Press

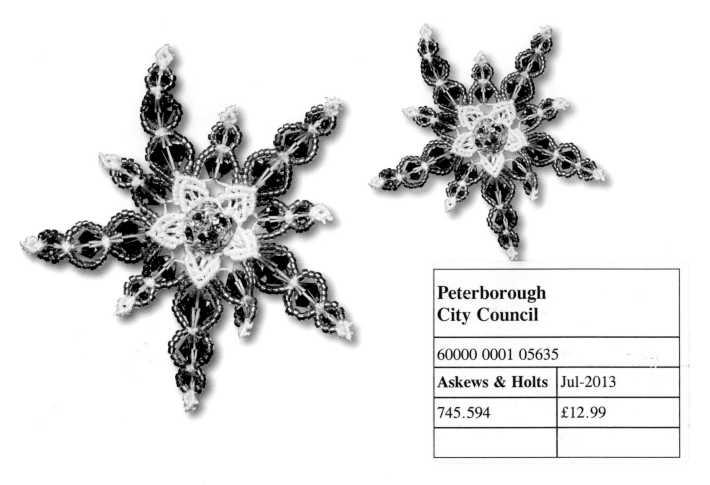

First published in Great Britain 2010 by Search Press Limited,
Wellwood, North Farm Road, Tunbridge Wells, Kent TN2 3DR

Originally published in 2009 as 'Micro-Macramé. 30 beaded designs for jewelry
using crystals and cords' by St Martin's Press, 175 Fifth Avenue, New York, N.Y. 10010

ISBN: 978-1-84448-549-9

Suppliers
If you have difficulty in obtaining any of the materials and equipment mentioned in
this book, then please visit the Search Press website for details of suppliers:
www.searchpress.com

Photography by Jules Doyle and Annika deGroot
Illustrations by Linda Shaffer

This book is dedicated to my fellow textile artists
Tini Jöns, Deepika Prakash, Karin Mantefors, and Vibeke Vennemo.
Many, many thanks to Annie Pearson, JoAnn Dunn, Linda Lowe,
Linda Shaffer, Jules Doyle, and my brilliant agent, Regina Brooks.

Contents

Introduction

Ten years ago I spied an intricate beaded bracelet in a jewellery display case as I walked into a trendy gift shop one day. The bracelet was made of undulating rows of beads and pearls, with some sort of silky cord peeking through here and there. Its palette ranged from lilac to deep dark cobalt blue, as if heaven had melted from one hue to the next. It was Shambhala, Narnia, Ys and Shangri-la, all wrapped up together. I was smitten.

Its construction was fascinating, too; what technique the artist had used to make this magical blend of beads, pearls and crystals was an utter mystery. Unfortunately, it was far out of my price range, so I returned to the shop every few months, hoping it would go on sale. One day I came back and it was gone.

Memory of it grew in my mind until it became something mythical beyond my reach, an elusive strange snippet of paradise I glimpsed once, a long time ago.

A few years later while surfing the Internet, I hit upon a beading site with pictures of a necklace in the same style – links on the Web page led to a lesson on how to create this micro-macramé neckpiece. *Micro macramé*. So that's what it was. It didn't look like the macramé I knew from my childhood in the 1960s. It had nothing in common with those chunky knotted plant hangers with fuzzy ponytails, or pop-eyed jute owls clutching barked twigs in their gnarled talons. It was macramé done on a miniature scale, with beads and crystals knotted together in undulating rhythms of colour.

Micro macramé is simply a return to an earlier form of macramé, one that precedes the sixties fervour for oversized, rustic knotted visual comments on how the times they were a-changin'.

A century or so ago macramé lace was all the rage; fashionable ladies macraméd wallets, pillowcases, and the ends of their shawls and towels with diminutive knotted dancing figures and labyrinthine combinations of double half hitches, square knots and tassels. They even macraméd lockets of hair in those dour glass-fronted mourning pins so prevalent in Victorian times! A century before *that*, sailors spread macramé knotting techniques the world over, port by port, as a way to make a little extra pocket money aboard ship and while away the time.

We lose track of the history of macramé before the fifteenth century, but we know the word *macramé* is an old Arabic word for 'towel' and that it predates the bobbin lace forms.

Micro macramé is a modern interpretation of an ancient art form. It takes macramé lace one step further by adding sparkly seed beads, fire-polished Czech and Austrian beads, and Swarovski glass beads to thin nylon or silk cords. Micro macramé is usually knotted into jewellery pieces, but can be used as edging for scarves, or for creating fancy clutches and evening bags.

This book focuses on creating micro-macramé jewellery items, from earrings to necklaces, with a few odd items thrown in for the fun of it. The first ten projects are simpler than the later ones and feature basic square-knotted bracelets and necklaces, three types of earrings, a hat or lapel pin, a mobile phone charm and a glitzy glam ring. By the tenth project, you will have worked all of the types of knots used in this book.

The ten intermediate projects introduce the concept of modules and working in the round. The final ten projects are even more advanced and cover roundels, using cabochon focal pieces, and knotting from the centre My hope is that these lessons in knotting will serve as a springboard for your own artistic creations.

—*Annika*

Beads, Lots of Beads

A good deal of the subtle sparkle in a micro-macramé piece comes from seed beads. The sizes most commonly used are 11 (11/0), 8 (8/0) and 6 (6/0). Sometimes beads can be found in sizes 9 and 10, and they work well in micro macramé; however, size 15 (15/0) is too tiny a bead to pass a micro-macramé cord through.

LARGER-FACETED BEADS such as fire-polished glass beads, which are manufactured in Austria, the Czech Republic and China, are available in sizes from 3mm up to 12mm.

SWAROVSKI GLASS BEADS feature prominently in micro-macramé jewellery. The Swarovski glass beads used in the projects in this book range in size from 3mm to 8mm.

Be wary of using semiprecious stone beads – always be sure to check the size of the holes bored into the beads and the 'sharp' edges of those bead holes. They can sever cording and snag it easily. Pearls, too, can pose a problem, since their holes are usually far too tiny for micro-macramé cords. However, they are easier to ream than semiprecious stones.

OJIME are boxwood beads from Asia that are carved in the shapes of animals and mythical creatures. They make excellent focal points for necklaces, as do lampwork glass beads.

BUTTONS, too, can be used as centrepieces, but are more commonly used as fasteners for necklaces and bracelets.

CABOCHONS AND CAMEOS can be glued on to scraps of ultrasuede and framed by lines of seed beads.

OJIME BEADS

BUTTONS

CAMEO

SWAROVSKI
GLASS BEADS

SEED BEADS

Cords for Micro Macramé

There are several options for the cord used in knotting micro macramé; some people adore waxed linen, which I find too sticky. Others use silk cord, which is sleek and soft to the touch, but is not for beginners since it is hard to remove knotting mistakes. Here are my picks:

TUFF CORD from Eurotool, my all-time favourite, is composed of three strands of long nylon fibres. It doesn't stretch, fray or shred. It can be used to string beads without a needle. All the cords here can be used without needles, but I prefer Tuff Cord because it is very forgiving when you have to pull out knots made by mistake. I use the no. 3 cord for most of my work; it is 0.4mm (0.0162in) in diameter and can hold tinier beads and crystals than any of the other cords (except for Stringth). I also use no. 5, which is 0.5mm (0.0216in) in diameter; it is very close in size to Conso, Mastex and C-Lon. Tuff Cord comes in sixteen colours in many diameters; stick with the no. 3 and no. 5 for best results.

STRINGTH comes in eleven colours and seven different sizes. I've used the no. 3 (0.4mm; 0.016in diameter) and no. 5, which is equivalent to the no. 5 in Tuff Cord and the no.18 in Conso, Mastex and C-Lon.

BEADSMITH 'no stretch' nylon beadstring no. 6 is another favourite. It is equivalent to the Tuff Cord no. 3. BeadSmith also supplies nylon no. 18, which is a larger diameter (5mm; 0.2in) and was originally used for hand stitching for the upholstery industry, but it, too, is very forgiving and flexible. It comes in nineteen colours.

MASTEX nylon no. 18 is used in the upholstery industry and has been around for a long time. It comes on cardboard spools. It has a lovely even twist and its colours seem a little shinier and truer than other types of cords. Its diameter is approximately 5mm (0.2in) and it comes in twenty-four colours. I have found it to be a little bit brittle on occasion, depending, I guess, on the dye lot.

C-LON BEADING CORD comes off the bobbin with some curl to it. You can either iron strands of C-Lon on your iron's lightest setting, or as you unspool it, wind off an arm's length at a time and pull it taut – this seems to take care of the unruly curl. Its diameter is just under 0.5mm (0.02in) and it comes in sixty-four colours.

> It may not be possible for you to find exactly the same beads and cords that the author has used. This should not deter you, however, from finding something equally attractive or useable. Nylon micro macramé thread or any beading cord, even waxed cord, can be used for all of the projects in this book. All of these are readily available from bead shops, internet sites or by mail order.

TUFF CORD

C-LON BEADING CORD

CONSO is an old standby that is the same diameter as C-Lon, Mastex and BeadSmith and is roughly the same diameter as Tuff Cord no. 5 and Stringth no. 5. It holds knots really well and can be washed with a toothbrush if it becomes a little funky. It comes in twelve colours.

GUDEBROD makes some terrific silk cording that can be used for micro macramé. It is, however, quite unforgiving if you tend to make frequent knotting mistakes and need to untie a lot of knots. Their silk cords come in over forty colours. Try the FF (0.38mm; 0.015in) and FFF (0.42mm; 0.0165in) sizes. They are wholesale only, so you'll have to shop around for a distributor.

SPARKLE ELASTIC can sometimes be found in large craft stores in the children's art section. Look for elastic cord in widths of no more than 0.5mm – if you can't find it that small, consider using larger beads with larger holes. Westrim Crafts supplies a 1mm gold elastic cord (manufacturer style: 176.4) and a 1mm silver elastic cord (manufacturer style: 176.3) that will hold 8mm beads.

DARIA MULTI YARN produced by Noro isn't actually a cord; it's a type of yarn. This multicoloured corded yarn is a little too large for the Swarovski and fire-polished beads, but makes nifty wallets or bags for mobile phones and iPods. It looks and works for knots like a thin version of mousetail.

DMC EMBROIDERY FLOSS comes in a zillion colours and is unforgiving as far as untying bad knots goes, but DMC floss is very pretty when knotted into bracelets, and it can hold beads as small as size 8 easily. It is commonly used for friendship bracelets.

WIRELACE 2.5MM MESH WIRE RIBBON is used as the holding cord in the **Paristan necklace.** It is fun to play with because the larger sizes expand up to three times their original width, stretching into all sorts of lacy, leafy, seaweedy shapes. WireLace comes in several widths – 1mm, 2.5mm, 6mm and 20mm. The 2.5mm WireLace is available in seven colours from Alacarte Clasps.

SPARKLE ELASTIC

CONSO

DARIA MULTI YARN

WIRELACE MESH WIRE RIBBON

Tools

You will need a good pair of **NEEDLE-NOSE PLIERS**, **SHARP SCISSORS** for cutting cord ends and a **CRIMPING TOOL** for crimping beads and clasps on to necklace ends.

DENTAL FLOSS THREADERS make great makeshift large-eyed needles for pulling cords through tight places like the spring bars of watchstraps.

REAMING TOOLS are used to enlarge the holes in ojime beads and pearls.

A SINGEING TOOL is a great addition for sealing the ends of synthetic cords. Many macramé aficionados routinely singe the ends of their nylon cords with an open candle or lighter flames. I find this daunting since it's too easy to slip up and melt too much cord, ruining the outer layer of knots. I prefer using a battery-powered singeing tool like Eurotool's BeadSmart Perfect End Thread Burner or BeadSmith's Thread Zap to cauterise cord ends.

NEEDLE-NOSE PLIERS

Another valuable singeing tool is a lit stick of incense; use the glowing end to melt cords and cover up that nasty burnt nylon smell at the same time! I only singe the ends of pieces that are knotted in dark-coloured cords; singeing will leave a hardened bit of black residue on the cords' ends which can be masked by the dark cord. Also note: You cannot singe the ends of silk or cotton cord and expect them to melt – singeing only works for nylon cords!

FRAY CHECK, a clear nail polish or clear glue is recommended to seal the cord ends of lighter-coloured projects and cotton and silk cords. In some cases even this measure is not ideal since the polish can discolour the knots a little, depending on the type of cord used. However, it is important to seal the knots in some manner to keep them from fraying and unravelling.

THE HUMBLE STRAIGHT PIN is one of the best tools you can have. Pins with long shanks, like quilting pins, can be used to pick out mistied knots, stabilise your micro macramé to a surface, or as a guiding tool for cinching overhand knots close to beads.

A PADDED CLIPBOARD is needed to anchor your knotted pieces as you work. (See following page.)

CRIMPING TOOL

SINGEING TOOL

REAMING TOOLS

How to Pad a Clipboard

Materials

- 40.5 × 37cm (16 × 14½in) piece of low-loft batting (available in the quilting section of fabric and craft stores)
- 56 × 58.5cm (22 × 23in) piece of white or unbleached muslin
- US Letter- or A4-sized clipboard
- Several long straight pins or safety pins

1 Lay the low-loft batting over the muslin, centred on top. Fold one 7.5cm (3in) edge of the muslin over the batting and smooth it out.

2 Flip the batting and muslin over and tuck the folded end under the clip of the clipboard.

3 Flip the clipboard with the batting and muslin over to its back and fold the bottom of the fabric up over the clipboard. If you don't want the padding to extend over the back, unfold the muslin and trim the batting closer to the edge of the clipboard, then fold the fabric back over the edge of the clipboard.

4 Fold one side of the fabric over and secure it to the bottom layer of fabric with a straight pin. Bury the sharp tip of the straight pin in the padding.

5 Fold the other side of the fabric over the back of the clipboard and secure it to the opposite side of the fabric with straight pins. Pull the fabric snug as you pin it down. Bury the points of the pins into the fabric so that there are no sharp points sticking out the back. If you like, you can substitute safety pins for the straight pins.

6 The clip in the clipboard can be used to secure loose cords while you are knotting a piece.

I have always used a padded clipboard as a surface to work micro-macramé pieces. There are other types of macramé boards available, but I prefer to work with a padded clipboard. The instructions here are for a US letter-sized clipboard (216 × 279mm; 8½ × 11in), which is similar in size to A4 (210 × 297mm; 8¼ × 11¾in), but shorter than US legal sized (216 × 356mm; 8½ × 14in). Experiment to see which is the most comfortable to you; the difference can affect how your upper back feels after an hour of knotting.

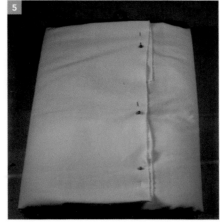

Sewing Beads Around Cabochons and Cameos

Placing a row of seed beads around a cabochon or cameo will frame it nicely for a finished look.

Start by gluing the cabochon on to a piece of ultrasuede or light felt. Thread a beading needle with beading thread such as Nymo and knot it tightly at the end of the thread. Come up from the underside of the ultrasuede as close as you can to the cabochon. On the upper side of the ultrasuede, thread five seed beads on to the needle and shape them around the side of the cabochon before sewing them down to the ultrasuede.

You'll want to backtrack a few beads and bring the needle up between the second and third beads. Thread the needle through the third, fourth and fifth beads, then add five more beads on to it and sew the beads down to the ultrasuede, following the edge of the cabochon.

Again, push the needle up between the second and third beads, thread it through the last three beads, and add five more beads before sewing them as close to the cabochon as possible. Continue this all the way around the cabochon. Tie off the thread with a knot on the underside of the ultrasuede. Clip the thread. Carefully cut away the excess ultrasuede, making sure you do not cut into the threaded line of beads.

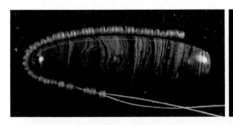
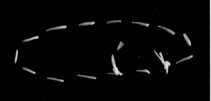

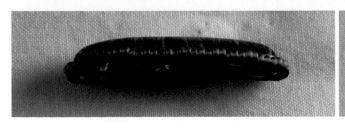
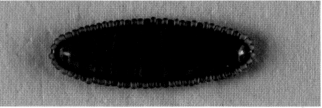

Knots Used in Micro Macramé

"It's too intricate for me! I could never get through an entire piece!" I hear that a lot from friends who've watched me knotting bracelets. Well, I'm about to let you in on a little secret: Macramé is deceptively easy to do and it goes a lot faster than knitting socks, scarves or sweaters. Most macramé work is based on a handful of knots: the lark's head, overhand, half hitch and double half hitch. Throw in the ever-popular flat knot (also known as the square knot), and you've got a complete repertoire.

LARK'S HEAD KNOT

We'll start with something simple: the lark's head knot. The lark's head is made by folding a cord in half and threading the loose ends of the cord through the loop formed by the fold.

 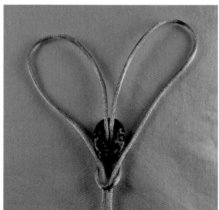 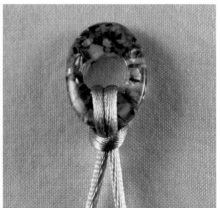

Lark's heads are used a lot to mount cords on to another cord to start a micro-macramé piece.

You can tie lark's head knots on to starting cords and then flip the knotted pieces over and work the rest of the knots from there; the backs of lark's head knots have a cleaner look and are less obtrusive.

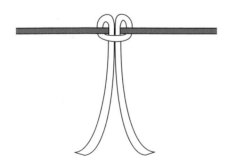  

FRONT   **BACK**

OVERHAND KNOT

An overhand knot is formed by simply making a loop in the cord and passing the end of the cord through that loop and drawing it tight. You can use a straight pin to position the knot close to a bead.

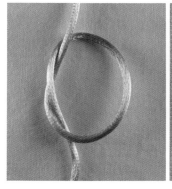   

An overhand knot can be made with more than one strand of cord, as in the two-strand overhand knot on the left.

HALF KNOT

A half knot is simply one half of a square (or flat) knot. In micro macramé, you tie half knots around inner cords. As you tie a continuous line of half knots, they will naturally start to twist around their centre cords, creating a downward spiral.

To make a half knot, place the right-hand cord in front of the filler (inner) cords, then thread the left-hand cord over that right-hand cord, behind the two filler cords, and back up over the right-hand cord. Pull those outer cords snug up against the inner cords. You've just made one half knot. Repeat that threading sequence again, place the right-hand cord in front of the filler cords, then thread the left-hand cord over that right-hand cord, behind the two filler cords and back up over the right-hand cord. Pull the outer cords tight. You've tied another half knot. As you continue to tie half knots, you'll see the line of knots spiralling around the enclosed centre cords. Seven half knots will usually create one full revolution of knots around the centre cord.

If you start a half knot on the right hand side, make all of the knots on the right-hand side in the whole piece to get that spiral effect.

FLAT KNOT

A flat knot is basically a square knot. In micro macramé, you tie flat knots around inner cords, the same as for half knots. Generally a flat knot is tied using four cords; the two cords on the outside enclose the two inner cords. As with the half knot, there's no limit on how many inner cords you use; some projects require four or more inner cords. Flat knots can be used to enclose a lot of inner cords in a micro-macramé project.

To make a flat knot, start by making a half knot. Place the right-hand cord *in front* of the filler (inner) cords, then thread the left-hand cord *over* that right-hand cord, *behind* the two filler cords, and *back up over* the right-hand cord. Pull those outer cords snug up against the filler cords. You have completed the first half of the flat knot.

Now cross the left-hand cord *in front* of the filler cords and the right-hand cord *behind* the filler cords. Thread the left-hand cord from *front to back* through the loop formed between the right-hand cord and the filler cords, and thread the right-hand cord from *back to front* through the loop created between the left-hand cord and the filler cords. Pull the cords tight to form a flat knot that encloses the two filler cords.

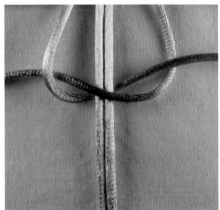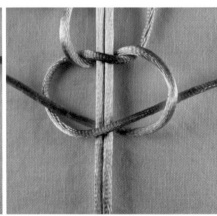

A line of flat knots tied one after the other will look like this:

ALTERNATING FLAT KNOTS

Alternating flat knots are frequently used in micro-macramé projects because they create a lacy-looking fabric base for watchstraps and bracelets. A bed of alternating flat knots can be worked on any number of cords divisible by four. For a bed of twelve cords, in the first row of knots, leave the outer two cords on both sides unknotted. Tie two flat knots, using two filler cords for each flat knot.

On the next row, use all twelve cords to tie three flat knots.

For the fourth row, repeat what you did for the second row – tie two flat knots, leaving the outer two cords on each side unknotted.

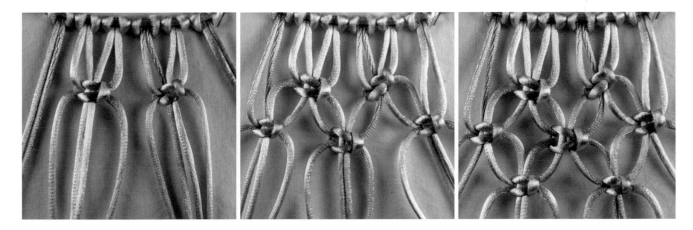

You can repeat this sequence again and again to create a fairly sturdy background for a button to be sewn on to.

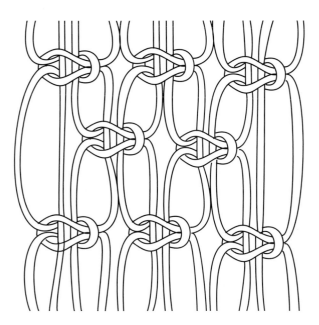

DOUBLE HALF-HITCH KNOT

Now we come to the double half hitch (sometimes known as the clove knot), which is as essential to micro macramé as the flat knot. Sequences of double half-hitch knots can be vertical, horizontal or diagonal. A vertical double half-hitch knot is achieved by wrapping a cord twice around a vertical filler cord.

In this book we'll use the diagonal double half hitch quite a lot. It is not an easy knot to learn for some people – myself included – but once you have mastered it, you can conquer the world! Here is how to start a sequence of diagonal double half-hitch knots that progress from upper left to lower right.

In the picture there is a line of six lark's head knots; each lark's head knot has two cords hanging down from it. Lay the farthest-left cord over all the other cords. This cord will become the 'filler' or 'holding' cord; that is, all of the other cords will be formed into knots that surround this cord.

From underneath the filler cord wrap the adjacent cord up and around it, threading the cord end through the loop, and pull that wrapping cord tight.

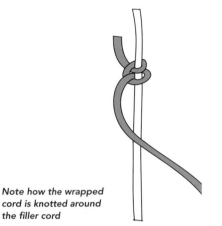

Note how the wrapped cord is knotted around the filler cord

Now wrap the same cord around the filler cord again and thread the end through the loop you created; these two wraps equal one double half-hitch knot.

The key is to keep tension taut on the filler cord when wrapping cords around that filler cord. Don't lose hope if this knot isn't easy to make. It takes a lot of practice to get evenly placed diagonal double half hitches. This can be daunting at first, so practise, practise, practise.

Here is a line of five diagonal double half-hitch knots that have been knotted from upper left to lower right. Now you can work on the right side.

To create a line of diagonal double half-hitch knots travelling from upper right to lower left, wrap the second-to-last cord on the right up and around the filler cord (rightmost cord), pulling the wrapping cord tight around the filler cord.

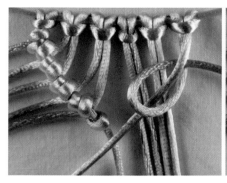  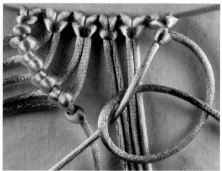

Wrap the same cord around the filler cord again and thread the end through the loop you created; you've now completed a right-sided diagonal double half hitch. Pick up the cord to the left of it and create another double half-hitch knot. Continue until you have created a line of them.

 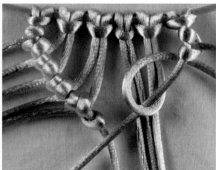 

To tie a line of left-side diagonal double half hitches and a line of right-side diagonal double half hitches to each other, cross the filler cord from the right-hand side over the left and use the filler cord from the left side to wrap a double half-hitch knot over it.

Another good thing to do is to use a straight pin to stabilise each section as you finish it. This really does make it easier to control how well the next double half-hitch knot falls into place.

Something Pretty Bracelet

This delicate bracelet features seed beads meandering around Thai Hill Tribes sterling silver origami beads. These unique pieces of origami are made of thin strips of silver folded into beads. If you cannot find them, you can use any type of 6mm glass bead such as Swarovski bicones or Czech or Austrian fire-polished glass beads.

This bracelet uses the double half-hitch knots. The double half hitch is the most commonly used knot in macramé and other lace forms such as tatting.

Materials

- Burgundy C-Lon cord (not C-Lon thread) or Tuff Cord no. 5, 136cm (54in) length × 1
- Large lobster claw clasps × 2
- 7 × 4mm sterling Thai Hill Tribes origami beads × 20
- Size-8 frosted pink seed beads, ½ tube
- Clear nail polish

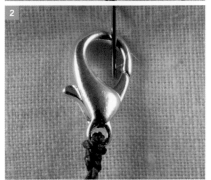

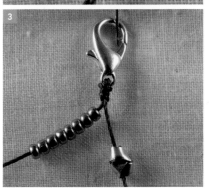

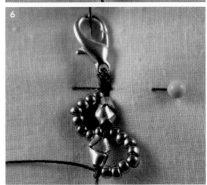

1 Measure off 46cm (18in) of the 136cm (54in) cord and fold the cord in two with one 46cm (18in) length and one 90cm (36in) length; make a lark's head knot, attaching the cord to the loop on the lobster claw clasp. Pin the clasp on to the padded clipboard with a straight pin.

2 Tie an overhand knot under the lark's head knot.

3 String a silver origami bead on to the 46cm (18in) length of cord, then string eight frosted pink seed beads on to the 90cm (36in) length of cord. To make stringing beads easier for yourself, trim the ends of the cord on the diagonal. If the cord's tips fray too much, coat them with a dab of Fray Check.

4 Using the cord strung with the frosted pink seed beads, tie a double half-hitch knot around the cord with the silver origami bead.

You have finished one section of the bracelet! Now all you need to do is create another nineteen sections.

As you can see in the picture above, the cord you used to string the frosted pink seed beads on to is shooting out to the right.

5 String eight frosted pink beads on to the cord and string a silver origami bead on to the shorter cord.

6 Tie a double half hitch under the silver origami bead with longer cord, as before.

7 Once you have completed the twentieth section, string the second lobster claw clasp on to the two strands of cord.

Tie it off with an overhand knot. You may want to use a straight pin to help guide the knot toward the clasp.

8 Tie another overhand knot and dab the cord with clear nail polish or glue.

Cut the excess cord away after the polish has dried. You can also singe the ends of the cut cord with a singeing tool or a lit stick of incense (beware that this may turn the ends of the cord black); this will melt the cords together. Be careful not to singe too much.

Try on your new bracelet and admire your supreme handiwork!

Owl Earrings

Here are some knotty owl earrings. These earrings use a series of diagonal double half hitches and beading to create a retro-inspired piece of jewellery. A very easy first project!

Materials

- Medium brown C-Lon Cord or gold Tuff Cord no. 5, 46cm (18in) lengths × 12
- 9 or 10mm O-rings × 2
- Size-11 green seed beads × 24
- 4mm green fire-polished beads × 4
- Sterling silver earwires × 2
- Needle-nose pliers (for attaching the earwires)
- Clear nail polish

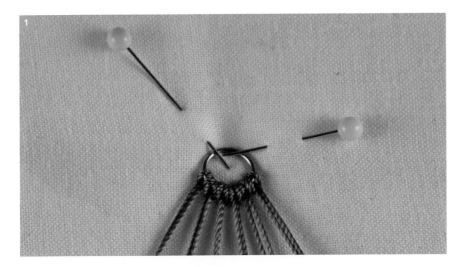

1. Fold six cords in half and tie six lark's head knots on to the first O-ring. Secure the O-ring to the padded clipboard with two straight pins.

2. Starting from the left side, start a series of five diagonal double half-hitch knots.

3. After you've finished them, tie a series of five diagonal double half-hitch knots from the right-hand side, to form both sides of a V.

4. Tie the innermost two cords together with a double half-hitch knot.

5. Tie another row of diagonal double half-hitch knots below this first row on each side.

6. Now we'll build the beak. Skip over the outer four cords on the left side and create two diagonal double half-hitch knots.

7. Skip over the outer four cords on the right side and tie two diagonal double half-hitch knots.

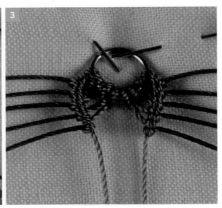

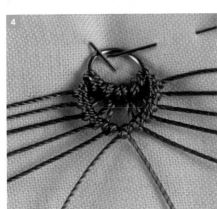

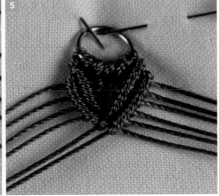

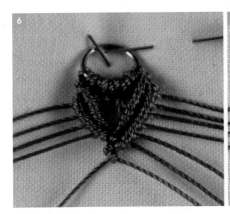

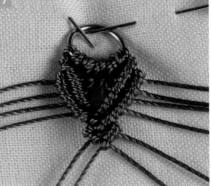

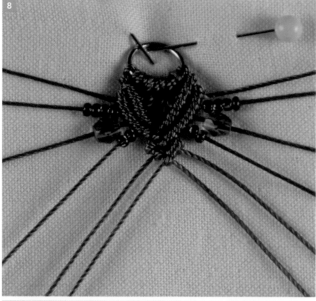

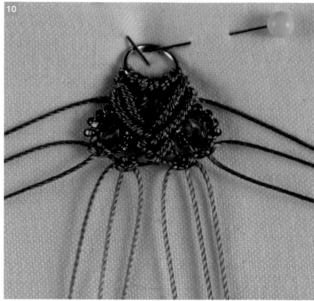

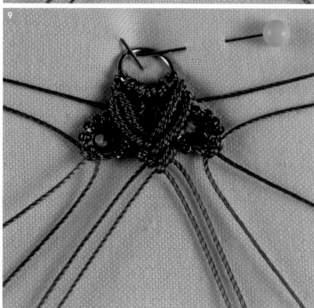

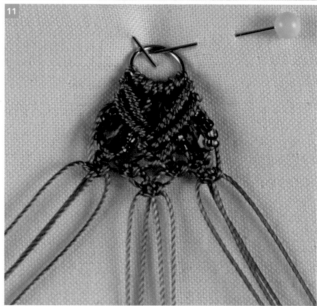

8   Now let's add beads for the eyes. From the left side, string four size-11 seed beads on the second-from-outermost cord. On the inner cord next to it, string a 4mm glass bead. Follow that with two seed beads on the cord to its right.

From the right-hand side, string four size-11 seed beads on the second-to-outermost cord, followed by a 4mm bead on the inner cord next to it and two seed beads on the cord next to that.

9   Tie a flat knot under each 4mm bead using the cords with the seed beads; the outer cords of this knot will enclose the two centre cords under the 4mm beads. You'll notice that the flat knots will be lopsided toward the side cords with only two seed beads on them. This is intentional.

10   Now we'll create the owl's body out of alternating flat knots. Take the two cords under the beak's left side and knot them in a flat knot with the innermost cord from the left eye. Most of the time we create flat knots with four cords; on these two knots we'll only use three cords – the two outer cords on each side are tied together in a flat knot enclosing the single central cord.

11   Create three flat knots using the leftmost four cords for one knot, the centre four cords for the second flat knot, and the rightmost four cords for the third flat knot.

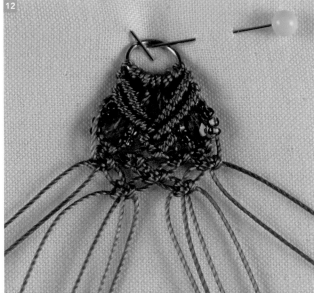

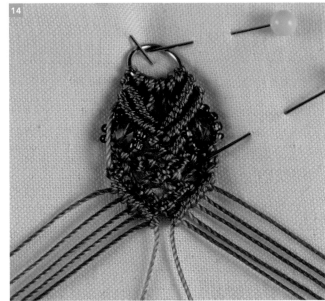

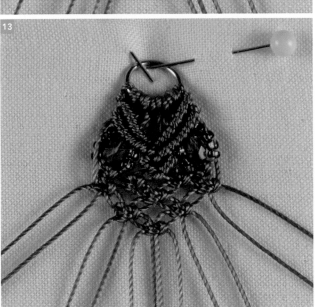

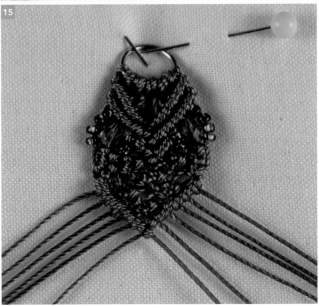

12 Tie two flat knots under these three knots by skipping the outer two cords on both sides and using the four innermost cords on the left side for one flat knot and the four innermost cords on the right side for the other flat knot.

13 Tie one single flat knot below the two knots using the central four cords.

14 Now let's add a row of diagonal double half-hitch knots to finish off the owl's body. Starting from the outermost left cord, create a row of five diagonal double half-hitch knots ending in the centre. From the outermost right side, create a row of five diagonal double half hitches meeting the left row in the centre.

15 Tie a final double half-hitch knot to unite the two sides.

Flip the owl over and dab the line of diagonal double half-hitch knots with clear nail polish. Wait for the polish to dry and clip or singe the loose cords close to the knots, making sure you don't cut into the knots themselves. Add an earwire to the O-ring at the top. Now build owl number two so you have a pair of them!

Icicle Earrings

Dots of light spiral down to a point of crystal – these dangly icicles are a cinch to make. Three types of knots are used: lark's heads, half knots and overhand knots. Half knots knotted together in a long row cause the cords to spiral. The decreasing spiral is produced by getting rid of two interior cords every few rows of half knots, until there are only two holding cords left inside.

You can easily vary the length of the icicles by snipping the inner cords every three or five half knots instead of every four, as shown in this project. Once you have mastered this technique, you can create a neckpiece of icicles suspended on a 2.5mm mesh wire ribbon (instead of on D-rings).

Materials

- 10mm D-rings or O-rings × 2
- Navy Tuff Cord no. 5 or blue C-Lon cord, 61cm (24in) lengths × 12
- Size-11 clear or white silvered seed beads × 1 tube
- 6mm barrel-shaped crystal beads × 2

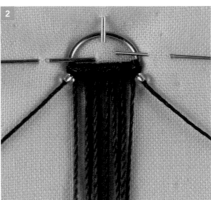

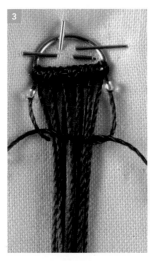

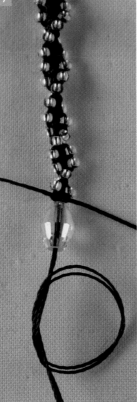

1 Fold six of the cords in half and use them to knot a line of lark's head knots on to the flat side of the D-ring. Secure the D-ring to the padded clipboard with a straight pin.

2 Thread a size-11 seed bead on to each of the outer two cords.

3 Now use these outer cords to tie a half knot, enclosing the inner ten cords within the knot.

4 Tie three more half knots around the inner cords by stringing each of the outer cords with one seed bead between each knot.

When you have tied four half knots, separate out two of the inner cords and snip them off close to the other inner cords. It doesn't matter which two inner cords you snip, you may choose any at random from this middle section, but be very careful with this step. Make sure you do not snip off the outer 'knotting' cords. You'll notice the icicle has already begun its spiral.

5 Tie four more half knots using a seed bead between the cords of each knot. Cut out two more of the middle cords, as above.

6 Continue with this pattern of tying four half knots with seed beads between the outer cords on each knot until there are only two interior cords remaining. Dab some clear nail polish on this last half knot and wait for it to dry before finishing the icicle.

7 String a 6mm barrel-shaped crystal bead on to the two interior cords and tie them off with an overhand knot.

8 Clip off the two 'knotting' cords above the barrel crystal bead. Dab the overhand knot with clear nail polish.

Snip the remaining cords when the polish has dried. Add an earwire to the D-ring at the top. Earring number one is finished! Follow the directions again to create your second earring. To make a mirror image of this spiral, knot your second earring left over right for each half knot, instead of right over left.

South by Southwest Earrings

The tiny wandering black veins in turquoise are striking when paired with black micro-macramé knots. If you don't have diamond-shaped cabochons, use oval ones to make these mesmerising earrings.

There are several ways to attach cords, cabochons and backings together. Often micro-macramé cords are wound so tightly on spools that when unwrapped they become snarled up together, making it hard to get them to lie flat. One of the simplest ways to tame them is to sew them into the backing; that way you can control the spacing of the cords, determining where each sits behind the cabochon.

Materials

- 21 × 18mm turquoise flat, diamond-shaped cabochons × 2
- Black fine-tip marking pen
- 7.5 x 5cm (3 × 2in) scrap of ultrasuede or thin felt × 1
- Black Conso cording or Stringth no. 5, 76cm (30in) lengths × 16
- Large-eyed sewing needle
- E6000 glue
- 8 × 5mm faceted jet teardrop beads × 2
- 8mm flat pad ear studs × 2
- Earnuts × 2
- Clear nail polish

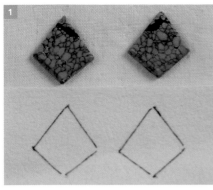

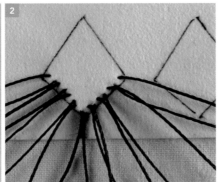

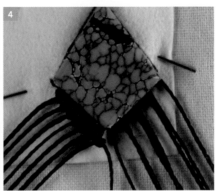

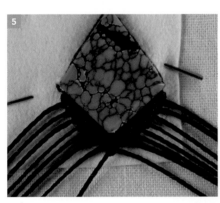

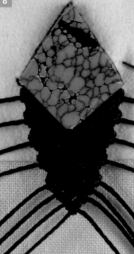

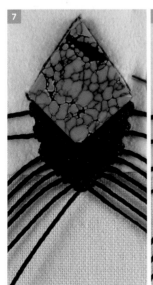

1 Trace around both turquoise cabochons with the black marker on to the scrap of ultrasuede or felt.

2 One by one, sew eight of the 76cm (30in) cords inside the markings along the bottom edges, leaving both tails of the cords hanging down.

3 Separate the tracings but don't cut close to the markings. Pin it to the padded clipboard. Put some glue inside the markings and carefully place the cabochon on top of the sewn-in cords. Let the glue dry.

4 From the left side, tie a row of seven diagonal double half-hitch knots.

5 Complete this row by tying eight diagonal double half-hitch knots on the right side. For the eighth knot use the holding cord from the left side as the wrapping cord for the holding cord from the right side.

6 Separate the outermost cords from both sides and pin or tape them out of the way. Tie a row of diagonal double half-hitch knots from the left and right sides.

7 Separate the outermost cords from this last row and pin or tape them back. Tie another row of diagonal half hitches on both sides.

8 Separate the outer cords from both sides and pin or tape them back. Tie a row of diagonal double half hitches on both sides. Again separate the outer cords and tape or pin them out of the way. Tie one final row of diagonal double half hitch knots with the four remaining cords on each side. You should now have five descending rows of diagonal double half-hitch knots.

9 String a jet teardrop on to the innermost two cords and secure it with an overhand knot. Dab each outer knot with clear nail polish. When the polish is dry, cut off the excess cords. Alternatively, you can cut the cords close, then singe their ends. Glue the flat pad ear stud to the backing. You're done with the first earring. Follow the above directions to complete the pair.

Ojime Necklace

Ojime are carved boxwood beads of intricate beauty. There are many different ojime available today, from antique to brand new; all make delightful focal points for neckpieces. Because they are so delicate, I hesitate to use ojime for bracelets and other jewellery items that come into contact with lots of surfaces.

This also is a good project for leftover beads from other projects; I encourage you to use beads you already have in your stash. Mix and match different colours and sizes and try new things. If you cannot find a Chinese knot bead to sit under the ojime, use a lampwork glass bead instead – make sure its hole is large enough to pass at least six cords through. Or simply leave that bead out.

Materials

- Lilac BeadSmith cord no. 6 or purple Tuff Cord no. 3, 304cm (120in) lengths × 4
- 4 or 5mm dark green fire-polished glass beads × 12
- 10mm teal fire-polished glass beads × 2
- 8mm lilac fire-polished glass beads × 2
- 6mm teal Swarovski round faceted beads × 4
- Size-6 teal seed beads × 4
- Size-8 teal seed beads × 48
- 6mm turquoise AB Swarovski bicone beads × 2
- 16mm oblong paua shell mosaic beads × 2
- Size-11 pale blue Delica seed beads × 1 box
- 8mm pale teal oblong fire-polished beads × 2
- Ojime bead × 1
- 11mm Chinese knot bead or a lampwork glass bead × 1

OJIME BEADS

1 Find the exact middle of the cords. Tie a loose knot in the middle and secure this knot to the padded clipboard with a straight pin. Tie twelve flat knots down one half of the cords, using the two outer cords to enclose the two inner cords in a flat or square knot. All of the lengths of flat knots that serve as separators for the beads will be in twelve-knot increments.

2 Add a 4mm dark green bead to the two inner cords and tie a flat knot below the bead, using the two outer cords.

3 Repeat this five times, then undo the loose slip knot and tie six sections of twelve flat knots, each followed by a dark green bead, down the other half of the cords. Finish this section with twelve flat knots at each end.

Add a 10mm teal fire-polished glass bead to each end of the necklace cords.

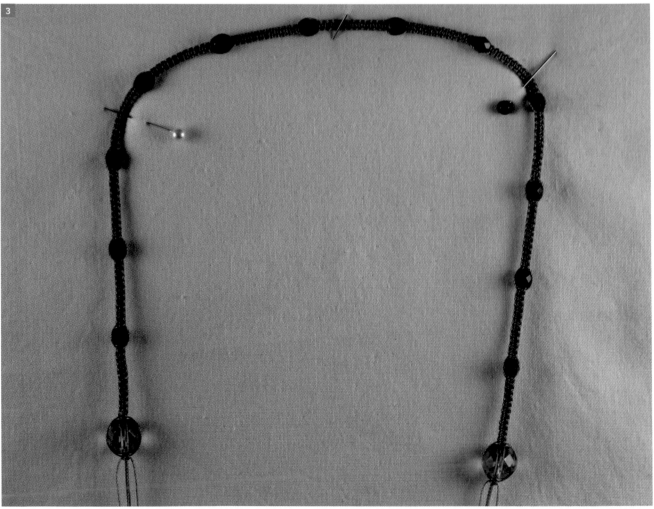

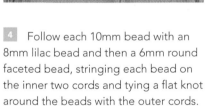

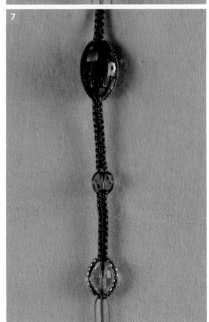

4 Follow each 10mm bead with an 8mm lilac bead and then a 6mm round faceted bead, stringing each bead on the inner two cords and tying a flat knot around the beads with the outer cords.

5 On the left-hand side create twelve flat knots, and then string a size-6 seed bead on the inner two cords and tie a flat knot around it. String six size-8 seed beads on each of the outer cords and string one 6mm turquoise bicone on to the centre cords. Tie a flat knot. String another size-6 seed bead on to the two inner cords and tie a flat knot around it. Do the same for the right-hand side.

6 For each side of the necklace tie twelve flat knots then string an oblong paua shell mosaic bead on to the two inner cords and tie a flat knot around it with the two outer cords.

7 Tie twelve flat knots then add a 6mm Swarovski round faceted bead to the two inner cords and tie a flat knot around it. Tie another twelve flat knots. String eight size-11 Delica seed beads on each of the outer cords and a 8mm oblong crystal bead on to the two inner cords. Tie a flat knot around it with the outer cords. Do the same for the other side of the necklace.

8 Tie sixteen flat knots on each side of the necklace, then string the cords through the ojime bead. If you cannot get all eight cords through the hole in the ojime, either ream the hole a little larger or carefully cut off two cords, one from each side of the necklace.

9 Tie an overhand knot right below the ojime bead. Now string the Chinese knot bead on to the cords and tie another overhand knot.

String 24 size-11 Delica seed beads on to each remaining cord, then add a size-8 teal seed bead and another size-11 Delica seed bead. Knot each cord with an overhand knot. Dab each cord end with clear nail polish. Wait for the polish to dry thoroughly, then clip the cord ends close to the overhand knots.

Fish Fob

No matter where you are in the world, this fish fob is a fun dangly little accessory to add to your mobile phone or iPod, or as a fashionable zipper pull on your favourite hoodie. String a school of them together on a necklace interspersed with semiprecious stone chips and dub your new creation 'Fish and Chips'. Have fun thinking up new ways to present these dappled underwater darlings.

Materials

- Teal Tuff Cord no. 3, 76cm (30in) lengths × 6
- Mobile phone mini-lanyard with split ring × 1
- 4mm green Czech fire-polished glass bead × 1
- Size-11 green seed beads × 22
- Clear nail polish

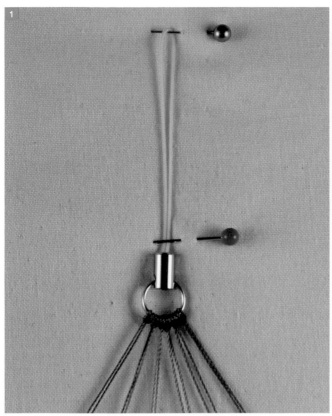

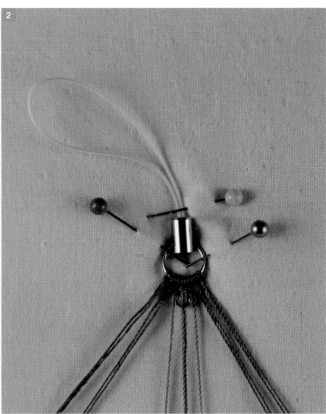

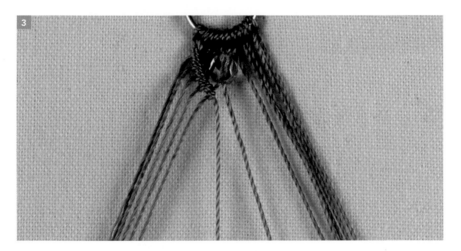

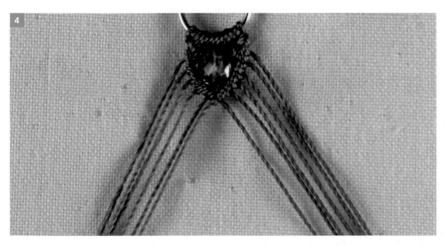

1 Fold the six lengths of cord in half and tie lark's head knots on to the split ring of the mobile phone lanyard. Pin the lanyard to a padded clipboard with straight pins.

2 String the 4mm fire-polished glass bead on to the centre two cords.

3 Starting from the left, tie a row of diagonal double half-hitch knots to enclose the bead. End on the sixth cord in from the left (remember, the holding cord you are wrapping with the other cords is cord number one).

4 Then from the right-hand side, tie a row of diagonal double half hitches ending on the sixth cord in from the right. The holding cord on this side is the rightmost cord.

Tie the two innermost cords together using a diagonal double half-hitch knot.

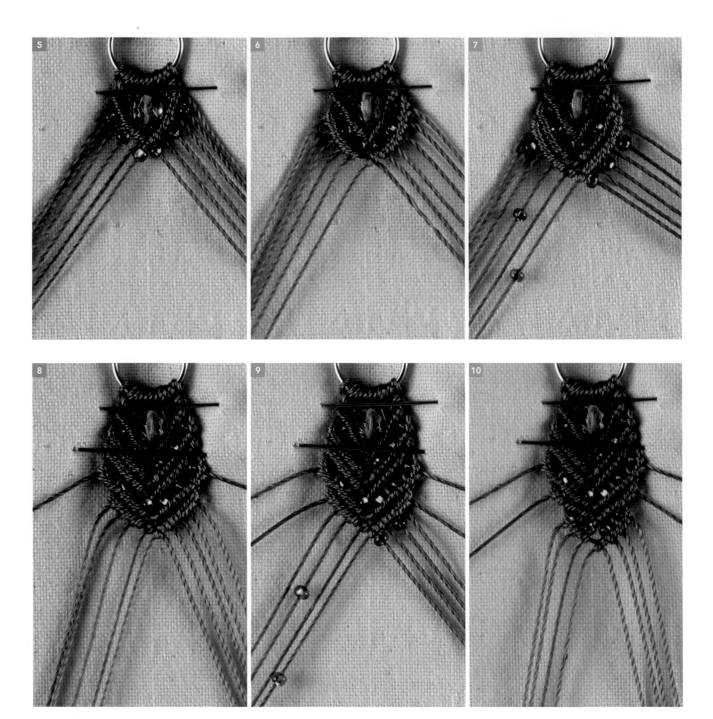

5 Numbering the cords from the left, string one seed bead on cords two, four and six. Do the same for the cords on the right side.

6 Enclose these seed beads with a row of diagonal double half-hitch knots on both the left and right sides. Tie the cords together in the centre with another diagonal double half-hitch knot.

7 Tie another row of diagonal double half-hitch knots. String seed beads on cords two, four and six on both sides.

8 Tie another row of diagonal double half-hitch knots.
Now we will begin decreasing the sides of the fish as we head toward its tail. Separate out the outermost cord on both the left and right sides and pin or tape them out of the way. Starting with cord two on both sides, tie a row of diagonal double half-hitch knots.

9 String a seed bead on to cords four and six on both sides. Separate out cord two on both sides and pin or tape it out of the way.

10 Starting with cord three on both sides, tie a row of diagonal double half-hitch knots, ending in the centre.

11 Separate out cord three on both sides and pin or tape it out of the way. Starting with cord four on both sides, tie one row of diagonal double half-hitch knots, bringing them together at the centre to create a V-shape.

12 Now we'll commence building the fish tail! Create another row of diagonal double half-hitch knots on each side but do not tie the two sides together in the middle. String a seed bead on to cord five on the left and right sides.

13 Enclose the seed bead with a diagonal double half hitch starting with cord four and ending with cord six. Do not tie the two sides together in the middle.

String another seed bead on to each cord five.

14 Enclose it with a diagonal double half-hitch knot, starting with cord four. Repeat this sequence one more time until you have three layers of single seed beads on each side of the fish's tail.

15 Tie a final row of diagonal double half hitches on each side of the tail.

Seal the knots with clear nail polish. While you are at it, seal the end knots on all the loose cords. Wait for the polish to dry, then clip all the cords close to the knots.

Victorian Hat or Lapel Pin

This pin features a diminutive agate cameo of Christopher Columbus's cargo ship, *Santa Maria*, celebrating the opening of the New World. It is comprised of jet beads enclosed in a single type of macramé knot and may serve as a great starting point on your voyage into micro macramé.

Materials

- Black Tuff Cord no. 3, 61cm (24in) lengths × 3
- 4cm (1½in) square scrap of ultrasuede × 1
- 17mm round cameo × 1
- Size-11 dark blue or black Delica beads × 1 box
- 5 × 7mm teardrop jet beads × 2
- 4mm round faceted jet AB fire-polished beads × 2
- Clear nail polish
- Size-12 beading needle or sewing needle
- Nymo or regular sewing thread
- 3mm oval jet AB fire-polished beads × 14
- 11.5cm (4½in) hatpin component × 1
- E6000 glue

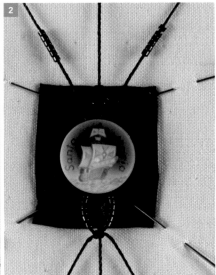

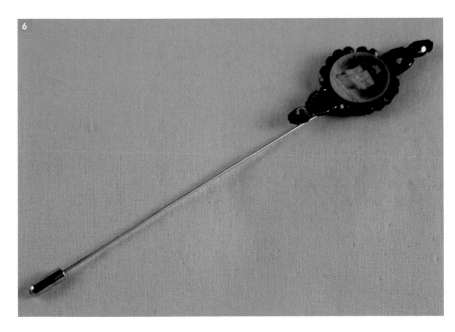

1 Sandwich the three cords between a scrap of ultrasuede and the cameo. Glue the layers together. You won't want to cut away the excess ultrasuede until the 3mm jet beads are sewn around the cameo in the final steps. Using straight pins, secure the scrap of ultrasuede to the padded clipboard.

2 On one side of the cameo, thread six Delica beads on to the two outer cords. Thread a 5 × 7mm teardrop jet bead on to the middle cord and tie a flat knot around it with the two outer cords. Do the same on the other end of the cameo.

3 On each side of the cameo, thread a 4mm round faceted jet AB bead on to the inner cord and tie a flat knot. Dab clear fingernail polish on these knots and clip the cords close to the knots.

4 Starting from the back of the ultrasuede, poke the threaded needle through and slide seven size 3mm oval jet AB beads on to the needle. Sew the beads on to the edge of the cameo (refer to page 9). Tie off the thread by knotting on the underside of the ultrasuede. Clip the excess thread. Do the same for the other side of the cameo.

5 Very carefully cut off the excess ultrasuede, making sure you do not cut into the sewing thread or beads surrounding the cameo.

6 Glue the hatpin component on to the back of the ultrasuede.

Got Rocks Ring

If you are lucky enough to find a supply of sparkly elasticised cord – check out the children's section in large craft stores – you can create lots of colour variations of this splashy adjustable accessory. Don't feel limited to using high-end crystal bicone beads – this ring will sparkle plenty no matter what beads you choose.

We'll start with building the ring's band out of elastic cord, then loop the cords back through the beginning knots of the band and string crystal beads on each cord, finishing with overhand knots to secure the beads.

Materials

- Sparkle cord, 1mm in diameter or less, 61cm (24in) lengths × 4
- Crystal beads × 8 – choose a variety of 4mm, 6mm and 8mm beads
- Clear nail polish

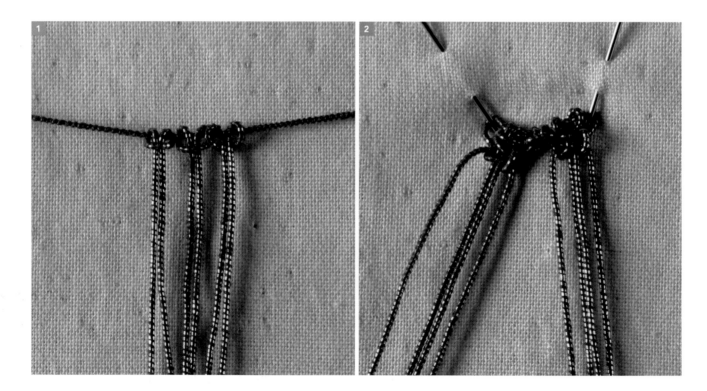

1 Use three of the cords to tie lark's head knots on to the fourth cord.

2 On the outer sides of the three lark's head knots, secure the fourth cord to the padded clipboard with straight pins. Tie one row of two flat knots, using four cords per knot.

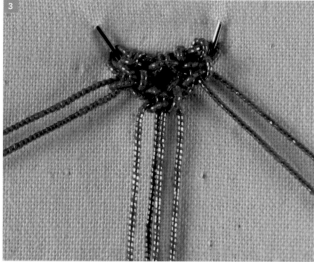

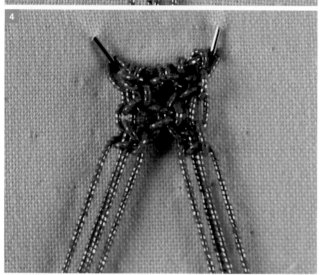

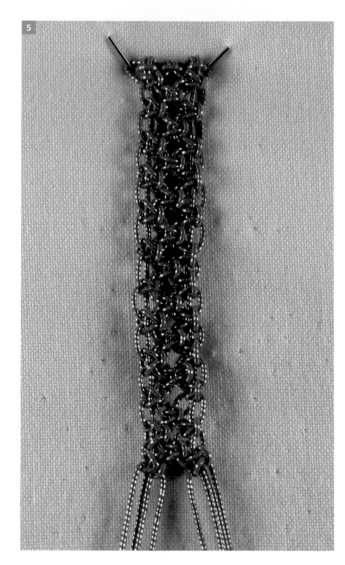

3   Then tie one flat knot in the next row using only the four innermost cords. The outer four cords will 'float' this row.

4   The third row will be made of two flat knots, made with four cords per knot, using the two centre cords, two outside cords.

5   The fourth row will be one central flat knot flanked by four floating cords. Follow this four-row pattern for 6.5cm (2½in). End on a row of two flat knots.

6   Take the outermost four cords and thread them through the holes left by the straight pins.

7   Now take the loose inner four cords and thread them through holes left between the flat knots at the start of the ring band. You may want to use a piece of cork or a large tube of seed beads to hold the round shape of the ring band as you work. Pull on ends to tighten.

8   Now thread a crystal bead on to each of the eight cords.

9   Slide each bead down to the ring band and secure it with an overhand knot. Dab the overhand knots with clear nail polish and clip the ends of the cords close to the beads. Try on your new glitzy glam ring!

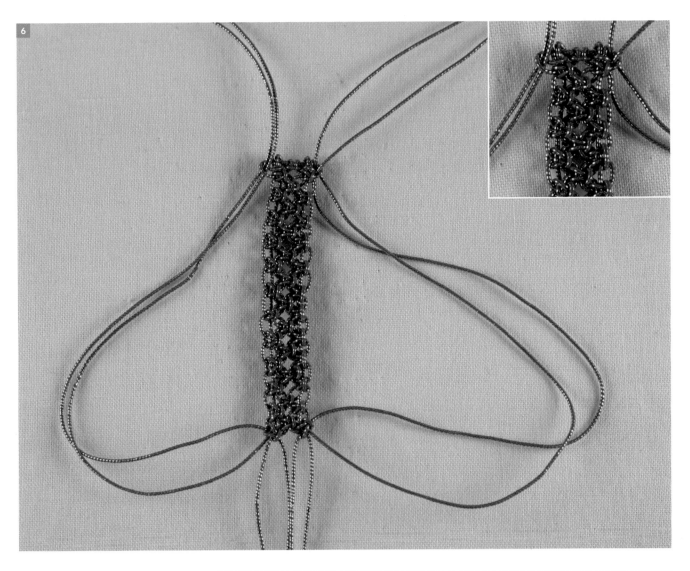

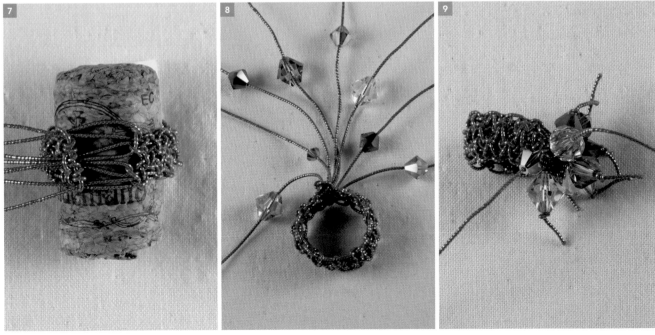

Glass Bead Bracelet

These days there are hordes of lampwork glass beads at art shows, high-end craft shops and even online. There are many shapes and styles available, from tiny globes that look like minuscule paperweights, to graceful fluid glass snippets made to float on gossamer neckpieces, to bobbly, bubbly cacophonies of colour.

Whichever style takes your fancy, remember to choose lampwork beads that have holes large enough to accommodate multiple strands of cord.

Materials

- Green Tuff Cord no. 3, 127cm (50in) lengths × 3
- Size-11 seed beads × ½ tube
- Size-6 peridot seed beads × 14
- 11mm lampwork glass beads × 2
- Clear nail polish

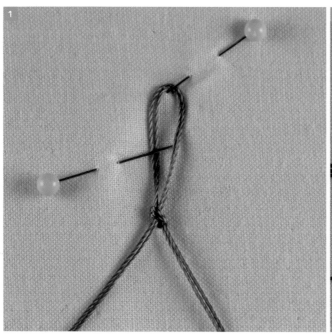
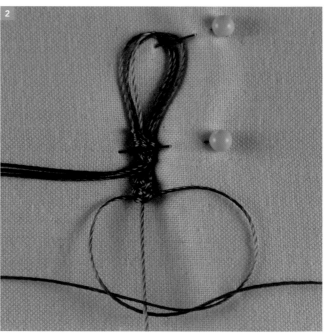

1 Find the middle of the three 127cm (50in) cords and tie a slipknot. Secure the slipknot to the padded clipboard with a few straight pins.

2 Below the slipknot, tie a flat knot with the three cords on the right side, using the two outer cords to enclose the inner cord between them. A flat knot here is simply a square knot that captures one inner cord.

3 When you have tied eight flat knots one after another, untie the slipknot; it was only there to get you started tying flat knots. Secure this line of knots with a straight pin.

4 Then tie another eight flat knots on the other side of the straight pin. Arc the whole row into a downward horseshoe shape to form the buttonhole fastening.

5 Take the two inner cords from the left end of flat knots and the two inner cords from the right end and tie them together in a flat knot. This will tie the buttonhole closed.

6 Using the outermost cords on the left and right sides, tie four flat knots, enclosing the inner four cords in each knot. Create a bead 'flower' by stringing four size-11 seed beads on to the outermost left cord and four more on to the outermost right cord. String one size-6 seed bead on to two of the inside cords from the flat knot; it doesn't matter which two as long as they are situated next to each other.

7 Place the other two inner cords behind the size-6 seed bead and tie a flat knot around them and the bead with the two outer cords.

8 You have completed one segment of the bracelet.

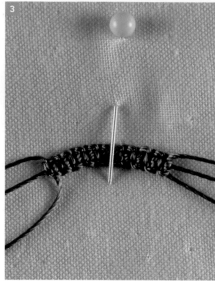

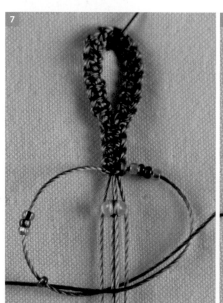

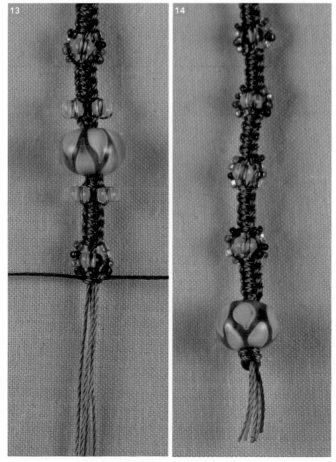

9 Follow the same instructions to create four more sequences of four flat knots followed by a flower of seed beads. Then tie four flat knots and slide a size-6 seed bead on to each of the tying cords.

10 Tie a flat knot below the size-6 seed beads.

11 String all four cords through the lampwork glass bead and tie another flat knot.

12 Slide a size-6 seed bead on to each of the outer cords and tie a flat knot below them.

13 Now follow the sequence at the beginning of step 6 again, to create five flowers with four flat knots between each flower.

14 Tie another four flat knots below this flower and slide another lampwork glass bead on to the four cords. Enclose it with an overhand knot. Dab the overhand knot with nail polish and wait for it to dry. Clip the ends of the cords close to the knot. Oh happy day!

Chopsticks

The most wonderful thing about wooden chopsticks is they're so *versatile*. You can nab a tasty morsel, or accent a fancy hairdo with them. I vote for the last option.

Most of the micro macramé here can be worked in the flat, but the fourth string of beads is knotted on to the chopstick. The tassel formed by tying a knot at the top of the chopstick is weighted by an assortment of beads; cloisonné, Swarovski butterflies, Czech fire-polished beads and seed beads.

Materials

- Red Tuff Cord no. 3, 61cm (24in) lengths × 16
- Size-11 orange or cherry seed beads × 1 tube
- 3mm bicolour light Siam Swarovski bicone beads × 16
- 6mm Siam Swarovski bicone beads × 16
- Wooden four-sided chopsticks with pointed tips at one end × 2
- An assortment of red, yellow and orange seed beads
- 4mm red round Cloisonné beads × 4
- 4mm red Swarovski butterfly beads × 4
- Glue

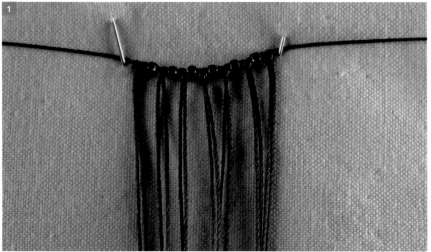

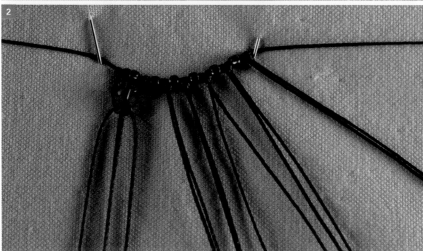

1 Fold seven cords in half and tie lark's head knots on to an eighth cord. Separate each lark's head knot with a size-11 seed bead, and secure the holding cord to the padded clipboard with two straight pins.

2 Working on the left side with the four outer cords (from the two leftmost lark's head knots), slide a 3mm bicone bead on to the two centre cords. Tie a flat knot beneath the bicone bead using the outer two cords.

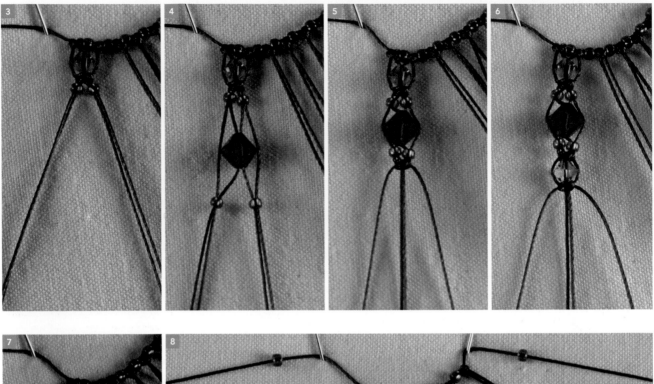

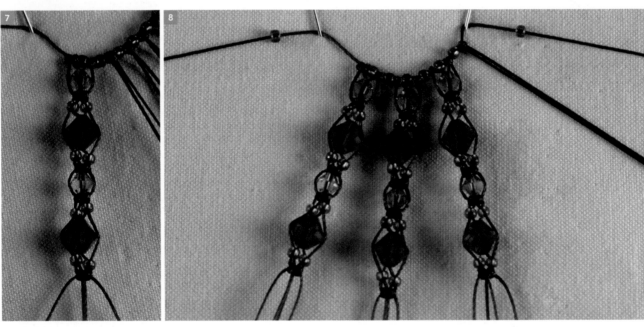

3 Working on just these four cords, string a size-11 seed bead on to each of the outer two cords.

4 Then string a 6mm bicone on to the inner two cords. Follow that with two seed beads on the outer two cords.

5 Tie a flat knot beneath them.

6 String another 3mm bicone bead on the inner two threads and tie a flat knot.

7 String a size-11 seed bead on each of the outer two cords, followed by a 6mm bicone strung on to the inner two cords, then two seed beads on the outer two cords. Tie a flat knot beneath them.

8 Repeat steps 2–7 on the next two lark's head knots, then again on the lark's head knots beyond them so that you have three sets of beaded lengths. At this point add a seed bead to either side of the holding cord.

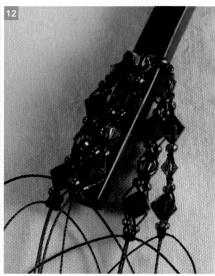

9 Take the piece off the padded clipboard and wrap it around the thick end of the chopstick, lining up the ends of the beads with the top edge.

10 Tie the two holding cords together with a flat knot.

11 Using the extra lark's head cord and the two holding cords, slide a 3mm bicone bead on to the two holding cords. Tie a flat knot beneath the bicone bead using the remaining two outer cords.

12 Repeat steps 3–7 to create another beaded length.

13 Using all the cords, tie an overhand knot at the top end of the chopstick and secure to the chopstick with a dab of glue. When the glue has set, you can twist the beads slightly around the chopstick to create a spiralling effect.

14 Add your collection of beads – cloisonné, butterflies, seed beads, bicones and fire-polished beads – a few centimetres down the ends of the cords and secure them with overhand knots and a dab of clear nail polish. Feel free to stagger the lengths of the cords a little to create depth. Clip the ends of the cords right beyond the knots.

Now create your second micro-macramé chopstick to make a pair.

Zigzag Bracelet

This zigzag bracelet features rows and rows of triangular beads cascading down tiers of diagonal double half hitches capped by a corded buttonhole and paua shell mosaic bead closure. There are three types of macramé knots used here, but the flat knot does double duty: first as a means of creating the buttonhole, then as a way to bring the knotted bracelet level.

Materials

- Green Stringth no. 3, 162cm (64in) lengths × 4
- Size-11 matte metallic dark abalone iris Toho triangle beads × 1 tube
- 10mm paua shell mosaic bead × 1
- Clear nail polish

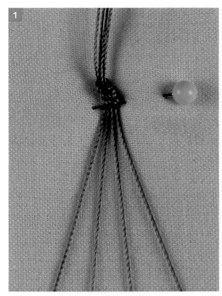

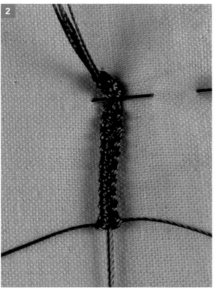

1. Find the exact middle of the cords, backtrack 2.5cm (1in) to one side, and tie a loose knot. Secure this knot to the padded clipboard with a straight pin.

2. Below this knot tie a flat knot, using two cords as the outer knotting threads. Continue tying flat knots until you have made eighteen of them. Unpin them and shape them into an arc. They now form the buttonhole for the closure bead. You don't necessarily have to make eighteen flat knots to form a buttonhole; how many depends on the size of the bead you've chosen. Just tie enough flat knots to encompass your bead.

3. Untie the loose knot made when you started – it was just there to hold everything in place until you were ready to finish the buttonhole. Secure the arced string of knots to the clipboard, bringing the two sides together.

4. Now you'll create a single flat knot in the centre that will bring the line of eighteen flat knots together, closing the loop, which becomes the hole for a button to pass through. Of the eight cords hanging down, separate them into three sections from the left: a section of two cords, a central section of four cords and a section on the right of two cords. Use the central section of four cords to create one flat knot, using the two outer cords to enclose the two inner cords in the flat knot.

5. On the next row, separate the row of cords into two sections of four each. Use the four cords on the left to tie a flat knot and the four cords on the right to tie another flat knot. As with the single knot above them, use the outer cords to enclose the two inner cords.

6. Below these two flat knots tie one flat knot with the centre four cords.

Paristan Necklace

Persian for 'fairyland', Paristan offers us a glimpse of an unearthly, shimmery fairy palace of graceful fountains and gardens. Azure and turquoise cords dance around the diamond-shaped frame of knots of this piece. Use this little window into fairyland to highlight your most magical beads and baubles.

Materials

- Pale turquoise Tuff Cord no. 3, 127cm (50in) lengths × 6
- Medium blue Tuff Cord no. 3, 127cm (50in) lengths × 6
- 2.5mm pale silver WireLace wire ribbon, 53.5cm (21in) length × 1
- 3mm AB fire-polished beads × 18
- 4mm blue zircon AB2X Swarovski bicone beads × 3
- 6mm turquoise AB2X Swarovski bicone crystal beads × 2
- 10mm blue AB teardrop-shaped Czech fire-polished crystal bead × 1
- Clear nail polish
- Silver metal crimp beads × 2
- Sterling silver bar and ring toggle clasp set × 1
- Crimping tool

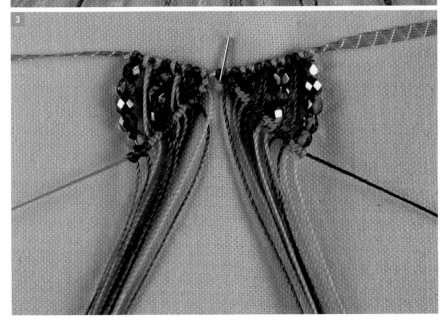

1 Fold each 127cm (50in) strand of cord in half and tie a line of twelve lark's head knots with them using the WireLace as the base cord. Alternate the medium blue and pale turquoise cords.

2 String five size 3mm fire-polished beads on to the two outermost cords on the right, then skip the next two cords and string three size 3mm fire-polished beads on the next two cords. Skip the next two cords and add one size 3mm fire-polished bead to the next two cords. Repeat on the left side.

3 Now you will create the diamond-shaped frame. Find the two central cords; the one on the left will be turquoise coloured and the one on the right will be blue. Use the turquoise one as the filler cord for a series of eleven diagonal double half-hitch knots that slant down toward the left. Use the lines of 3mm beads you strung in step 2 as a guide for how tight to draw each diagonal double half-hitch knot – each one should sit snug up under the beads above it. Then, starting from the central blue cord, create a line of diagonal double half-hitch knots that slant down the right-hand side.

The filler cord on the left side remains the filler cord for the next step, forming an L shape as you slant the next set of diagonal double half-hitch knots back toward the centre. Likewise, when you work the set of diagonal double half-hitch knots on the right side, they will mirror the L shape created on the left side.

Reynard's Leafy Lair Necklace

This elfin neckpiece can be accented by an antique pressed-glass leaf bead or the fairy charm of your choice. Instead of limiting yourself to just one of these pointed sections, why not consider stringing several of them side by side on to the same necklace?

The pattern of this necklace is a variation on a wallet from a Victorian macramé book. A 4mm dark green crystal is enclosed in each 'arrowtail'.

Materials

- Green Tuff Cord no. 3, 152cm (60in) lengths × 3
- Green Tuff Cord no. 3, 127cm (50in) lengths × 16
- 4mm leaf green Czech fire-polished beads × 10
- Size-8 leaf green hexagonal seed beads × 1 tube
- Medium pressed-glass green leaf beads approx. 11 × 13mm × 2, **or** use a sterling silver charm × 1 as the charm on the pendant and a 10mm leaf green Czech fire-polished bead × 1 as the button for the closure
- Clear nail polish

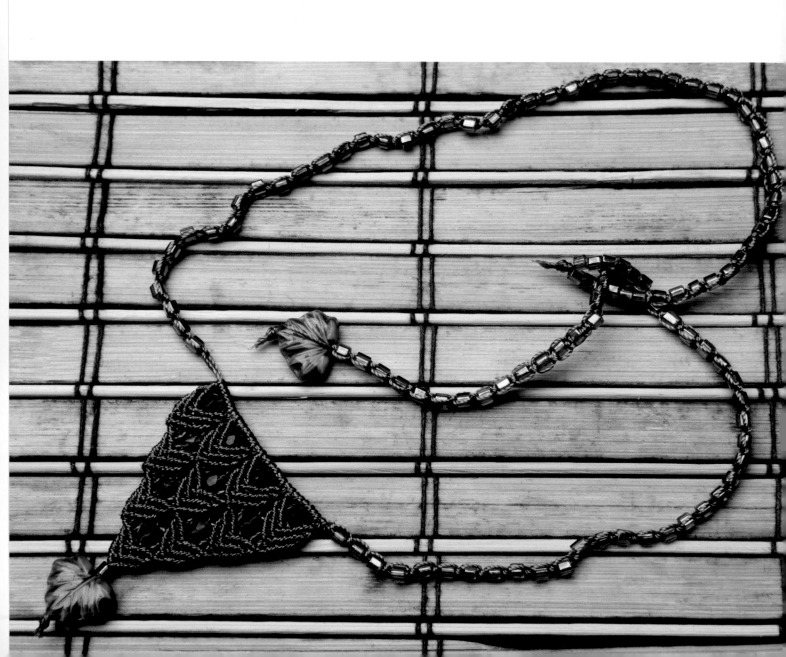

1 Fold the 127cm (50in) length cords in half and tie sixteen lark's head knots on to the three 152cm (60in) lengths of cord. Secure the cords to the padded clipboard with three straight pins, dividing the lark's head knots into four equal sections.

2 On one of the four sections, string a 4mm leaf green fire-polished bead on to the two innermost cords.

3 Using the outer cords in the section as holding cords, tie a row of diagonal double half-hitch knots around the 4mm bead.

4 Tie two more rows of diagonal double half hitches below that row.

5 Repeat steps 2–4 on the three other sections of cords.

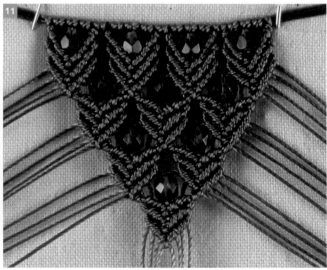

6 String a 4mm leaf green fire-polished bead on the outermost cords of the two central sections.

7 Tie a row of diagonal double half-hitch knots beneath the bead.

8 Tie two more rows of diagonal double half-hitch knots below this row. String 4mm leaf green fire-polished beads on the outer threads of the sections to the left and right of this central section.

9 Tie a series of three diagonal double half-hitch knots beneath each of these beads. String 4mm leaf green fire-polished beads on to the outer cords of the central section and its adjacent sections.

10 Tie three rows of diagonal double half-hitch knots beneath each bead. String a 4mm leaf green fire-polished bead on to the centre two cords.

11 Create three rows of diagonal double half-hitch knots below it.

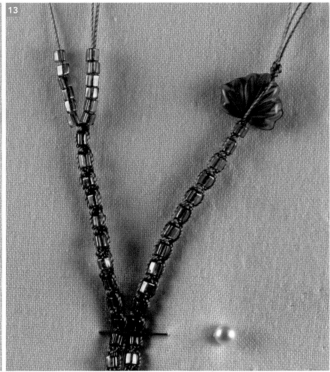

12 Turn the piece on its side to work on the necklace's holding cords. String a size-8 seed bead on to the middle cord and tie a flat knot around it with the two outer cords.

Repeat this for 20cm (7¾in). Turn the necklace over and work this same pattern on the other side of the holding cords.

13 On one end, separate the cords into two uneven halves; string six size-8 seed beads on to two cords, and six size-8 seed beads on to the other lone cord. Tie the two halves together with a tight overhand knot to create a buttonhole. On the other end, string a pressed-glass leaf bead on to all three cords and secure it with an overhand knot. Seal the knots with clear nail polish and wait for them to dry. Clip the ends of the cords.

14 String a size-8 seed bead then a pressed-glass leaf bead on to the two innermost cords at the point of the macramé piece and secure them with an overhand knot. Dab the knot with clear nail polish and let dry. Clip the ends of the cords. You'll also want to seal each of the cords on the sides of the triangular macramé section with nail polish and clip ends close to the knots.

Beaded Tassel

An inherited writing desk from my grandfather sported a forlorn-looking key dangling out of the lock in its drawer for as long as I can remember. The key was always in danger of getting lost or misplaced and needed a pretty tassel to make it more noticeable! This knotted tassel can adorn just about anything, from key chains to zipper pulls.

Working in the round is a little daunting at first. Only the final steps of tying the three sections together to enclose the tassel head are knotted on the actual tassel; the prior steps are worked flat on a padded clipboard.

A store-bought tassel was used for this project. There are several great sources for creating your own tassels online and in other craft books.

Materials
- Red Tuff Cord no. 3, 76cm (30in) lengths × 18
- Size-11 red seed beads × 1 tube
- 10cm (4in) store-bought gold tassel × 1
- Large-eyed sewing needle
- White glue

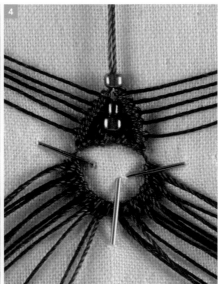

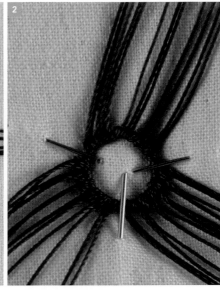

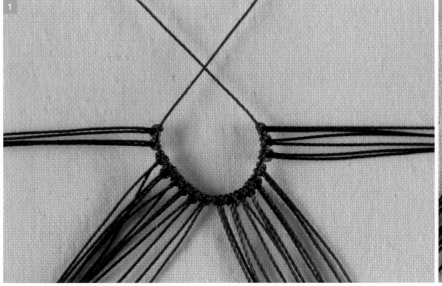

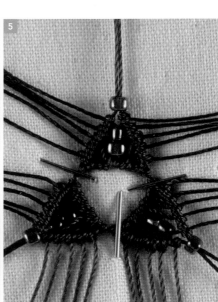

1 Fold seventeen of the cords in half and tie lark's head knots on to the eighteenth cord.

2 Tie the ends of the eighteenth cord together with a square knot. Separate the eighteen cords into two sections of six lark's heads and one section of five lark's heads with the square knot as one of the middle knots.

3 On the two innermost cords in one section, thread two seed beads.

4 Enclose the two beads with a row of diagonal double half-hitch knots, using the outermost cords as holding cords. Do not knot the innermost cords to each other. Instead, add a single seed bead on those two cords.

5 Repeat steps 3–4 on the other two sections of cords.

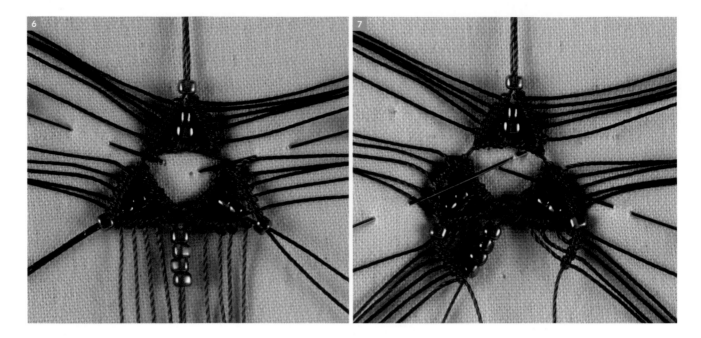

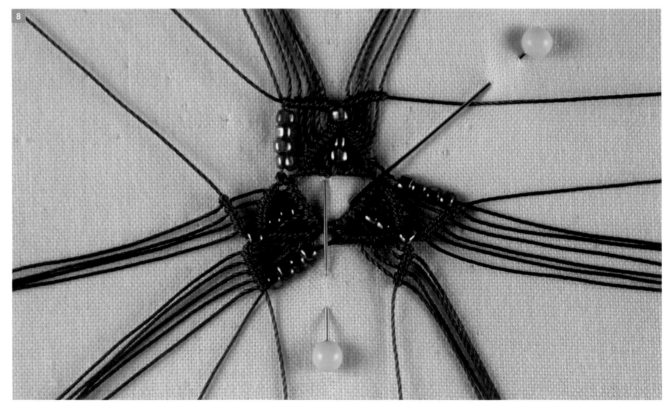

6 Using the outermost cords from two of the sections, string four seed beads on to both cords.

7 Tie a row of diagonal double half-hitch knots starting from under the single bead at the centre of the left section and ending with the cord under the four seed beads. Then tie a complementary row of diagonal double half hitches, starting from under the single bead on the right-hand side, ending on the cord to the right of the four seed beads.

8 Turn your padded clipboard so that the next section is easier to work on and repeat steps 6–7 on the other two sections of cords.

9 Take the piece off the padded clipboard; the rest of the piece is worked in the round. Slip the hanging cord of the tassel through the triangular opening in the centre of the piece and tie the adjacent holding cords of the diagonal double half-hitch rows to each other around the tassel using a flat knot. Add a single seed bead below each row of tied diagonal double half-hitch knots. You do not need to tie a knot underneath the seed beads, as the wrapping in the next step will secure the beads in place.

10 Wrap one of the cords hanging down around the tassel several times, securing the last few rows with a dab of white glue. Thread the cord on to the large-eyed needle and bury the cord deep within the head of the tassel. Clip the cord wherever it emerges from the tassel head. You can leave the other cords hanging to blend in with the tassel's own cords, or you can carefully clip them close to the wrapped cord.

Art Deco Watchstrap

Comprising rows of diagonal double half-hitch knots punctuated by a central row of sterling silver beads, this Art Deco–style watchstrap can be made in any colour to complement a range of watch styles. This timepiece, featuring a woven silver face cover, caught my eye at a local second-hand shop.

The closure on this watchstrap features a row of flat knots that fit snugly over inner cords that can be adjusted to fit tighter or looser. If you want a more traditional closure, you'll need to find a watch buckle and follow the directions for the Lady S. Timepiece on page 68.

Materials

- Red Conso cord, or red Tuff Cord no. 5, 127cm (50in) lengths × 12
- Found watch face with spring bars × 1
- 3mm round sterling silver beads × 30
- Black Conso cord, or black Tuff Cord no. 5, 30.5cm (12in) lengths × 4
- Glue
- Clear nail polish

1　Fold red cords in half and tie six lark's head knots on each of the watch's spring bars with the underside of the watch facing up.

2　Flip the watch over and tie a row of five diagonal double half hitches from the left. From the right, tie a row of five diagonal double half hitches. Don't tie the last cord on to the holding cord. String a 3mm silver bead on to the two inner cords to close this row.

3　Tie another row of five diagonal double half hitches from each side, tying the cords in the middle.

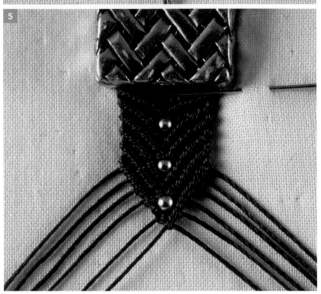

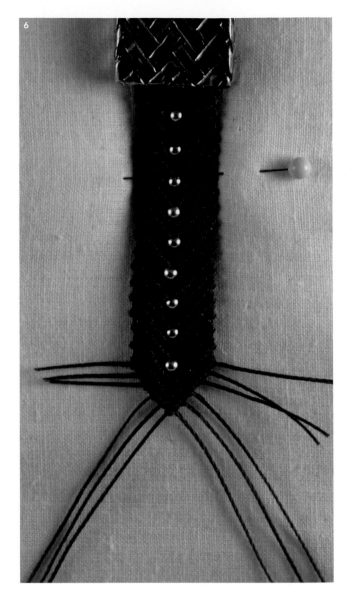

4   Tie the third row of five diagonal double half hitches from each side and use another 3mm silver bead to close this row in the centre instead of a knot.

5   Continue this pattern until you have created eighteen rows using nine of the silver beads.

6   Add two more rows of diagonal double half hitches. At this point you can snip off the outer three cords on both sides of the strap. You don't need to snip them close to the knots just yet, but it might help to keep the loose cords in order.

7   Well done! Now build the second half of the watchstrap on the other side of the watch face. When both sides are built, remove the watchstrap from the padded clipboard. Cross the six cords from one side over the cords from the other side of the strap and tie a flat knot around all twelve cords with the four black cords.

Use your fingers to brace the watchstrap as you tie the flat knots.

8   Or wrap the watchstrap around a small glass to tie the knots.

Tie three or four more flat knots with the black cords, wrapping all the red cords very tightly.

9   Use clear nail polish to seal the diagonal double half-hitch knots on the cords you cut off on the sides of the watchstrap. Clip cords close to the knots. Seal the black flat knot closure with glue to seal those knot edges; make sure you cover only the flat knots and not the red cords inside them. Once dry, clip the black cords close to the flat knots.

String a 3mm silver bead on each of the remaining red cords, and tie each off with an overhand knot. Dab the overhand knots with clear nail polish and after the polish has dried, clip the cords close to the knots.

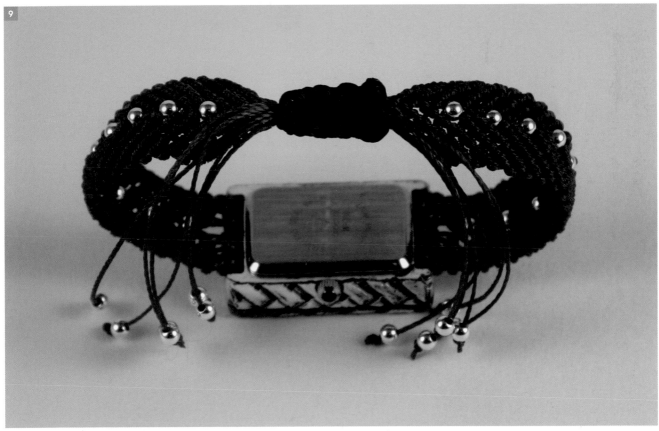

Lady S. Timepiece

Those who knew her will agree, my mother led a most remarkable life. Highly intellectual and only sometimes circumspect about it, she was a curious blend of scientist and social butterfly. Her eyes flashed sage green whether engaged in scholarly pursuit or dancing a fandango on the neighbour's coffee table. I will always miss her. This timepiece pays homage to her charmed brilliance.

Consider scouring local secondhand shops for old watches. Many of these watches end up in charity shops simply because their batteries need replacing. I always keep a ready supply of watch batteries at hand.

This exquisite Art Deco–style watch was a lucky find. I salvaged the original buckle and used it on the new watchstrap. If you don't have a watch buckle, consider using a buttonhole and an antique button closure instead.

Materials

- Turquoise Tuff Cord no. 3, 152cm (60in) lengths × 12
- Ornate silver-toned watch face × 1
- Size-11 nickel-plated matte sage/pewter iris Toho seed beads × 1 tube
- Size-11 green/blue/gold Miyuki no. 354 seed beads × 1 tube
- Size-10 blue/bronze Miyuki no. 1825 seed beads × 1 tube
- Silver-toned watch buckle × 1
- Small scrap of ultrasuede
- Clear nail polish

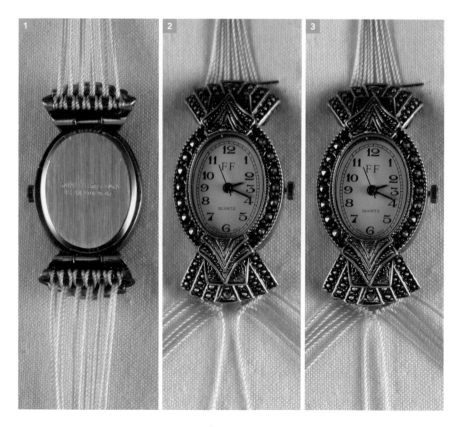

1   Fold the cords in half and tie six lark's head knots to each spring bar with the underside of the watch facing up. You may find it easier to thread the cords through the tiny space between the watch and the spring bar if you use a dental floss threader.

2   Flip the watch over and tie a row of five diagonal double half-hitch knots starting on the left-hand side and ending in the middle. Some of these knots may be covered by the edge of the watch. Then tie a row of five diagonal double half-hitch knots starting from the right-hand side and ending in the centre.

3   Tie the holding cords of the two lines of diagonal double half hitches together.

Diamond Girl Watchstrap

Diamond Girl is a regal talisman of prosperity and good fortune. Show and share your good luck by wearing this sparkling lady. She features bicones and seed beads nestled in-between layers of diagonal double half hitches and finishes up with a bed of lacy flat knots. There's no need to knot in adjustment holes for the buckle's tines to pass through since the flat knots have built-in openings on each row. A final touch of sparkle in the loop holds the tongue of the watchstrap in place.

Materials

- Red Tuff Cord no. 30, 127cm (50in) lengths × 12
- Queen of Diamonds watch face – check online auction sites for watches with playing card faces
- 4mm diamond AB Swarovski bicone beads × 6
- Size-11 silvered clear seed beads × 1 tube
- 3mm diamond AB Swarovski bicone beads × 8
- Gold-tone watch buckle × 1
- Red sewing thread, 51cm (20in) length × 1
- Clear nail polish
- Glue

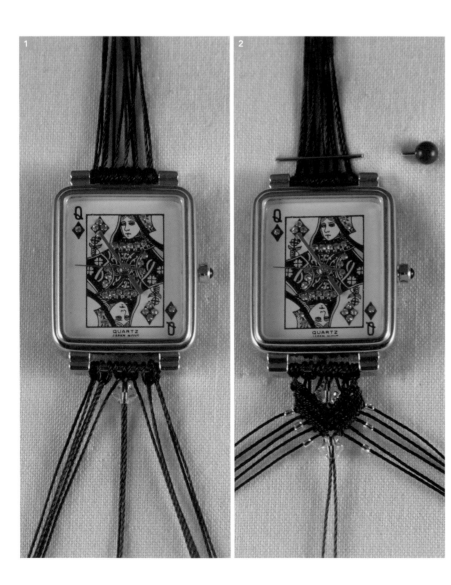

1 Fold the cords in half and tie six lark's head knots to the watch's spring bars on each side. String a 4mm diamond AB bicone bead on to the innermost two cords.

2 Starting from the left-hand side, create a row of diagonal double half-hitch knots ending in the middle. Starting from the right-hand side, tie a row of diagonal double half hitches ending in the middle. Tie two more rows of diagonal double half hitches below this row, but do not tie the innermost cords together on the third row.

Starting on the left-hand side, string a silvered clear seed bead on to the first cord, then the third, then the fifth cord. On the right-hand side follow the same pattern. Slide a 4mm diamond AB bicone on to the two centre cords.

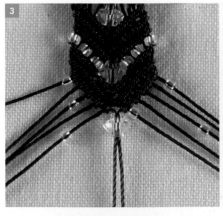

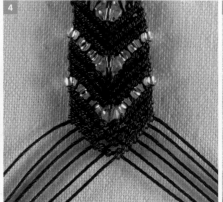

3 Tie three rows of diagonal double half-hitch knots below the 4mm bead then add six seed beads and a 4mm crystal bead in the next row as above.

4 Now tie three more rows of diagonal double half-hitch knots below the 4mm bead.

5 Using the outer four cords, tie a full knot on the left-hand side. Do the same on the right-hand side.

6 Tie two full knots below these knots, using the inner four cords on each side of the piece.

7 Now tie three full knots below these two knots.

8 Then tie two full knots below these three knots.

9 You'll continue in this pattern of two knots, then three knots, for 6.5cm (2½in), ending on a row with two knots.

10 Under the two knots, tie a single full knot with the four centre cords.

11 Starting from the left, tie a row of diagonal double half hitches down to the middle cord. Then tie a row of diagonal double half hitches from the right side. Tie two more rows of diagonal double half hitches. Dab clear fingernail polish on the last row of diagonal double half hitches and let it dry. Clip the cords close to the knots. You are done with this half of the watchstrap.

12 On the other half of the strap, follow steps 1–9 with the exception that in step 9 you will tie only 6cm (2¼in) of full knots. End on a two-knot row and tie one single full knot with the centre four cords below them.

13 Thread the watch buckle's tine through one of the holes above a central knot.

14 Flip the watchstrap over to its back and fold the remaining strap down on itself. Either sew the edges of the overlapped strap with red sewing thread, or glue the strap to itself using clear glue. Since this watchstrap is fairly see-through, I sewed the two layers together. Don't cut the sewing thread just yet.

15 Flip the watchstrap back over and, starting on one side, string eight size 3mm diamond AB bicone beads on to the sewing thread. You want a slight excess of beads to span the width of the watchstrap since you'll use this loop of beads to hold the watchstrap's two sides flat. Sew the end of the beaded loop to the other side of the strap and secure it with several knots. Dab clear nail polish on the knot at the end of the sewing thread and on the full knots on the underside of the watchstrap. When the polish is dry, clip all the loose ends, making sure you do not clip into a knot.

Cliffdweller Brooch

I love using natural and semiprecious stones in my macramé pieces but find that the holes in the stone beads are drilled haphazardly and are rarely large enough to accommodate anything but the slimmest nylon macramé cord.

Here an elongated rainbow calsilica cabochon is surrounded by turquoise-coloured seed beads and accented by 5mm azurite beads. The twisting cords beneath the cabochon look like ladders climbed by the brave souls who dwelt in cliffside caves. You probably won't be able to find a cabochon exactly like the one I used; this brooch can be made with a rounder cabochon and instead of nine sections of 'ladders' start with seven or five.

Materials

- 40 × 18mm rainbow calsilica cabochon × 1
- Scrap of ultrasuede
- Turquoise-coloured size-11 seed beads × 1 tube
- Size-12 beading needle
- Nymo beading thread
- Fawn Conso cord, 127cm (50in) lengths × 18
- Fawn Conso cord, 61cm (24in) length × 1
- 4mm or 5mm azurite or turquoise beads × 28
- 4cm (1½in) pin back with locking bar × 1
- Glue

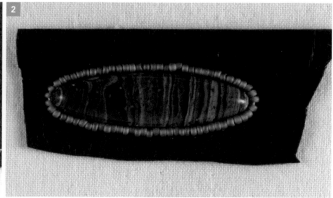

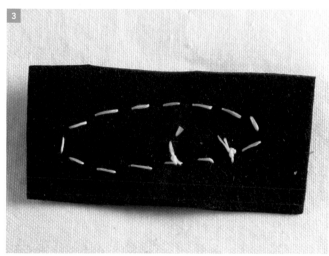

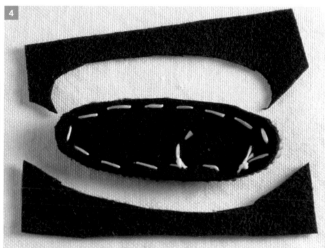

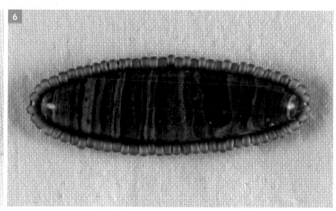

1 Glue the rainbow calsilica cabochon to the scrap of ultrasuede. Using a beading needle and Nymo thread (see page 9), sew the turquoise seed beads around the edge of the cabochon.

2 Complete sewing the turquoise seed beads all the way around the edge of the cabochon.

3 From the back of the ultrasuede, you can see that the stitching does not need to be perfect.

4 Carefully cut away the excess ultrasuede.

5 Make sure you do not cut into the Nymo thread or turquoise seed beads.

6 Here is the completed framed cabochon after trimming.

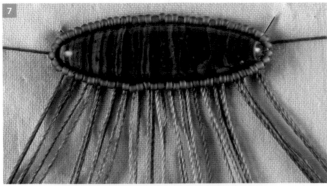

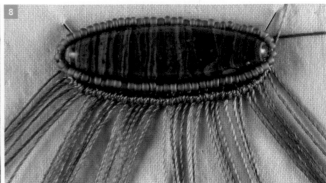

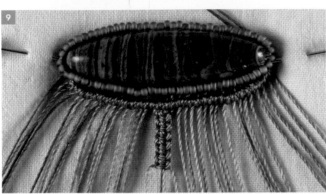

7 Fold the eighteen 127cm (50in) lengths of cord in half and tie eighteen lark's head knots on to the 61cm (24in) length of cord. Glue this line of lark's head knots to the back of the ultrasuede on the cabochon. Let the glue dry.

8 Starting at the left-hand side and using the leftmost cord as the filler cord, tie a row of double half-hitch knots around the lower edge of the turquoise seed beads surrounding the cabochon. Glue both the ends of the holding cord to the back of the cabochon.

9 Divide the cords into nine sections of 4four cords each. Tie the innermost section in a series of six flat knots.

10 On either side of this section tie a series of twelve half knots on each section. Alternate the sections by tying flat knots and half knots so that you end with five lines of flat knots interspersed with four sections of half knots.

11 Separate out the outermost cords on the left and right sides and leave them to the side. Then, on the right-hand side, take the two left cords from the outer section and the two right cords from the section next to it and tie a line of six flat knots.

12 Follow this with seven lines of flat knots on the other sections, each line six knots long.

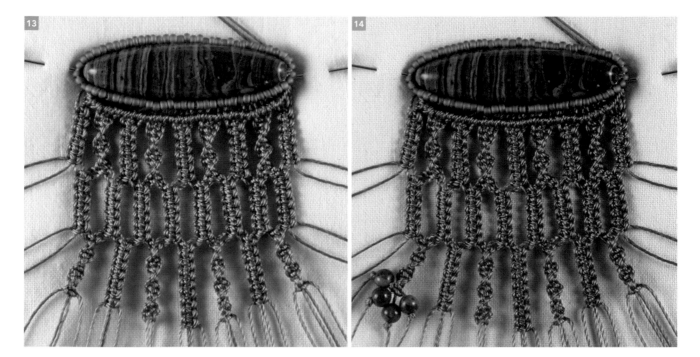

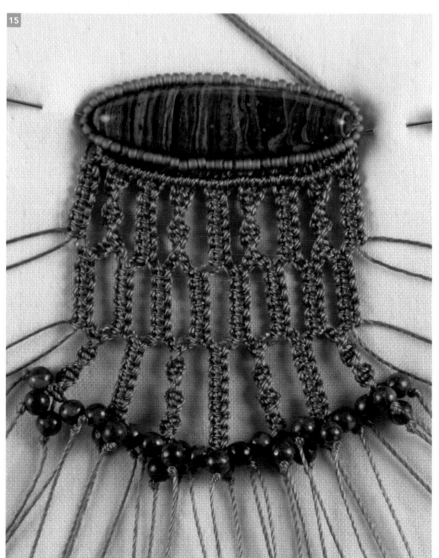

13 Separate the outermost cords on the left and right sides again and leave them to the side. Now tie seven lines of cords beneath this section of eight lines of flat knots.

Like in step 10, you will alternate full and half knot lines; however, the lines of half knots at the ends will be twelve half knots long, the two flat knot lines next to those will be seven knots long, the next two half knots will be sixteen half knots long, and the central line of flat knots will be nine flat knots long.

14 String a 5mm azurite bead on to each of the four cords in the first line of knots on the left side. Secure each bead with an overhand knot.

15 Continue with the remaining six lines of knots. Secure each bead with an overhand knot. Dab the knots with clear nail polish. Once the polish has dried, clip the cords close to the overhand knots. Glue the pin back to the ultrasuede behind the cabochon and let it dry.

Victorian Cameo Brooch

This elegant brooch is reminiscent of bejewelled Victorian tokens of remembrance and incorporates jet beads – a nineteenth-century favourite – with seed beads and an agate cameo. It is suitable for adorning a prim and proper business suit, evening gown or velvet frock coat lapel.

The seed beads are couched on to a backing of ultrasuede to frame the cameo, while the sides of the brooch are made up of flat knots surrounding jet beads and a latticework diamond made of diagonal double half hitches tipped by more jet beads.

Materials

- Black Tuff Cord no. 3, 61cm (24in) lengths × 12
- Scrap of ultrasuede
- Large-eyed sewing needle
- 18 × 25mm agate cameo × 1
- Size-11 dark blue or black Delica seed beads × 1 box
- Size-12 beading needle
- Black Nymo beading thread
- 6mm jet AB faceted Swarovski crystal beads × 2
- Size-11 jet AB seed beads × 1 tube
- 4mm jet AB fire-polished beads × 8
- 3mm jet AB fire-polished beads × 10
- 4cm (1½in) pin back × 1
- Glue

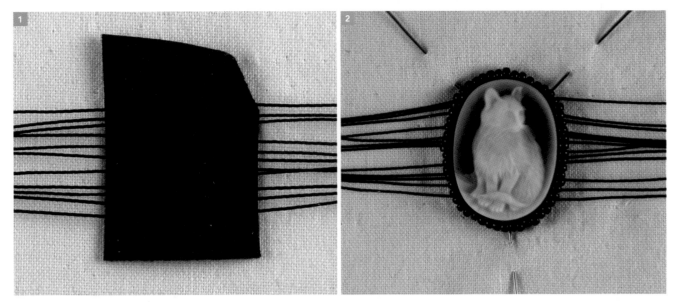

1 Anchor the twelve lengths of cord to the ultrasuede backing by sewing them through the scrap. Leave equal lengths of cord on either side.

2 Glue the cameo to the top side of the ultrasuede, covering the cords. Sew the black seed beads around the cameo (see page 9) and trim the excess ultrasuede off very carefully. Pin to padded clipboard.

3 Divide the cords into two sections of six cords on each side of the cameo. Create a row of diagonal double half-hitch knots with the twelve cords on each side.

4 String a 6mm jet AB faceted bead on to the centre two cords on each side; flank them with six jet seed beads on the adjacent cords. Tie a flat knot under each 6mm jet bead using the cords with the seed beads; the outer cords of this knot will enclose the two centre cords under the 6mm bead.

5 Now you're going to create beaded 'flowers' flanking the centre 6mm bead sections on either side of the cameo. String four jet seed beads on each of the outermost cords followed by one 4mm jet bead on the two cords next to them and four jet seed beads on the cords beyond that. Tie a flat knot around each 4mm jet bead.

6 Repeat with another set of four jet seed beads, 4mm jet bead, and four jet seed beads, and secure each centre bead with a flat knot. You'll find that the 6mm beads surrounded by the 4mm beads will seem a little crowded; nestle the clusters of beaded 4mm sections behind the 6mm beaded section.

7 Using the centre two cords as holding cords, knot outward creating a left and right row of diagonal double half hitches. Once knotted, the cords will naturally want to cross over each other; if you want to weave them in and out of each other, you certainly can, but it's not necessary.

8 Lay the left-side cords over the right-side cords and, using the outermost threads, tie a row of diagonal double half-hitch knots back toward the centre.

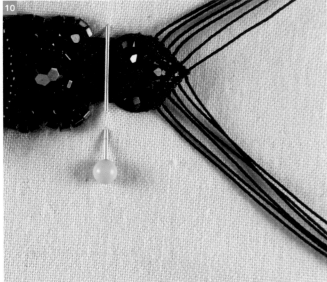

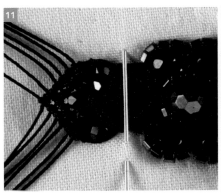

9 Starting with the second cord from the left, string a 3mm jet bead, then skip the third cord and string a 3mm jet bead on the next cord. String one 3mm jet bead on to the two centre cords, then skip a cord and string a 3mm jet bead on to the next cord, skip a cord and string a 3mm jet bead on to the next one.

10 Finish this sequence with two rows of diagonal double half hitches starting from the outside cords and working toward the centre. Seal the last row of diagonal double half-hitch knots with clear nail polish. Once the knots are dry to the touch, clip the cords close to the knots.

11 Finish the other side of the brooch the same way.

12 Glue the 4cm (1½in) pin back to the back of the ultrasuede.

Baroque Bracelet

This bracelet reminds me of Miami Beach before it became the top destination for supermodels, a time when the hotels still had velvet-flocked wallpaper and fountains adorned with blindingly whitewashed Greek statues.

It features round metal balls set with many-faceted crystals that look like tiny rhinestone wrecking balls, sunset pink–coloured seed beads, and your choice of Austrian, Czech or Chinese fire-polished crystals. Make sure these crystals have holes large enough to pass two cords through them.

Two types of macramé knots are used: the double half hitch and the flat knot. The diagonal double half-hitch knots can be left out in some places if you have trouble forming them.

Materials

- Gold Tuff Cord no. 3, 178cm (70in) lengths × 6
- Size-11 pink seed beads × ½ hank
- 3mm crystal bead × 10–12
- 8mm Swarovski rhinestone round beads × 7
- Size-6 hot pink seed beads × 1 tube
- 4mm Swarovski bicone beads × 1 tube
- Clear nail polish
- Fancy button
- Needle and thread

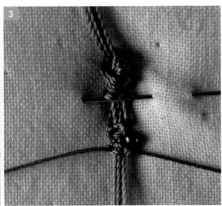

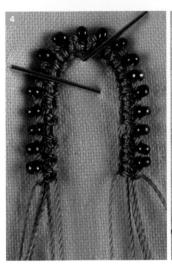

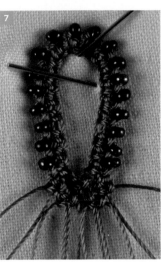

1 Find the exact middle of the cords, backtrack 2.5cm (1in) to one side, and tie a loose overhand knot. Secure this knot to the padded clipboard with a straight pin.

2 On one side of the knot create a flat knot, using two cords as the outer knotting cords.

3 Thread a size-11 seed bead on the right-hand side outer knotting cord and tie another flat knot.

4 Continue tying flat knots with seed beads on the right-hand side until you have made 18 of them. Unpin them and shape them into an arc. They now form the buttonhole where the button will pass through. You don't necessarily have to make 18 of them; sometimes 16 will do. It depends on the size of the button you chose. Untie the loose knot you made when you started – it was just there to hold everything in place until you were ready to finish the buttonhole.

5 You now have twelve cords to work with, six from each side. You'll use these cords to create a bed of alternating flat knots. That is, with the twelve cords you will create a row of three flat knots across, using four cords for each flat knot. Then, in the row below that, you will skip two cords, tie two rows of flat knots, and end with two unused cords on the other side. Below that row, you'll create three rows of flat knots, enclosing a 3mm crystal bead within the central knot. Below that row, you'll tie two flat knots, skipping the two cords on the outer sides. And finally, you'll tie one single flat knot below the crystal bead. This section becomes a V-shaped segment of the bracelet. So let's get started.

Take the two inside cords from each side to create a flat knot that will connect the left and right sides together. With these four inside cords, create a flat knot by tying the outer cords around the two innermost cords.

6 Now, using the four cords to the left of this central flat knot, tie another flat knot. Then, using the four cords on the right side of the centre flat knot, tie another flat knot. You've completed your first row of flat knots.

7 Tie a row of two flat knots. Remember to skip the first two cords on the left side; like the two outer cords on the right side that aren't used, they will 'float' this row.

8 For your third row of flat knots, separate your twelve cords into three sections of four cords each. String a 3mm crystal bead on to the two centremost cords. Tie a flat knot at the bottom of this crystal bead with the cords on either side of the bead.

9 Using the inside four cords in the left-hand section, tie a flat knot to the left side of this central knot enclosing the bead, then tie a flat knot on the right side using the inside four cords there.

10 Tie a row of two flat knots. Remember to skip the first two cords on the left side and the two last cords on the right side. Another row is complete. For your last row, tie a single flat knot using the four cords in the centre.

11 Now you will create a centre-slanting line of diagonal double half-hitch knots from both the left- and right-hand sides to form a V shape surrounding your segment of flat knots. Please note – this step is optional if you have trouble forming diagonal double half-hitch knots. Feel free to leave it out. Don't let yourself be frustrated by this step!

Use the farthest left cord as a filler cord for a series of five diagonal double half-hitch knots that start from the left-hand side and progress toward the centre point. Then tie a series of diagonal double half hitches from the right side using the outermost right cord as the filler cord for the five diagonal double half hitches that slant down to the centre. Remember that right-sided diagonal double half-hitch knots are formed opposite of the way you form left-side diagonal double half hitches. Refer to the instructions on how to create diagonal double half-hitch knots on pages 14–15. Now tie the two sides together with a double half-hitch knot using the left-hand cord as the filler cord for the right-hand cord.

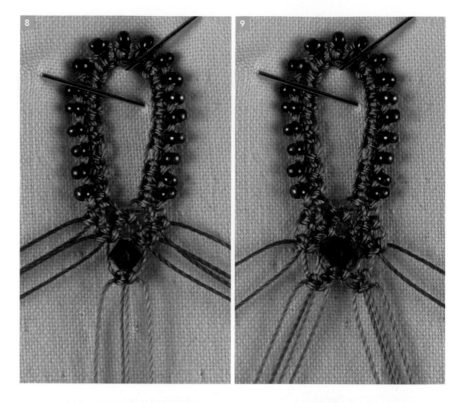

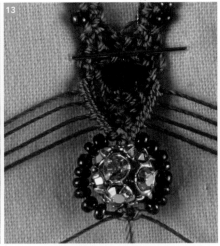

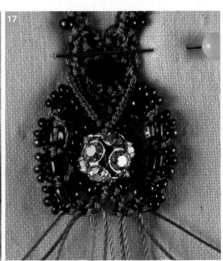

12 You are now ready to start building the first roundel of the bracelet. Separate your twelve cords into three sections. You may want to secure the first and last sections out of the way as you work on the middle section. String a rhinestone round bead on to the innermost two strands of cord. If you don't have rhinestone rounds, you can use any 8mm fire-polished glass beads; it is your choice. Use the cord on either side of the bead cords to string eight or so seed beads. You'll need to string enough of them to surround one half of the central bead. The number of seed beads you use depends on the size and shape of your central bead.

13 Now tie a flat knot under the central bead and the cords it is strung on with the two cords holding the seed beads.

14 Now let's create the sides of the roundel that frame the central bead. Each side is made up of four cords that are strung with three size-11 seed beads on their outer cords, one size-6 seed bead on the two inner cords and no beads on their inner cords. By leaving a bead off the inner cord, you can arc the finished side around the central section, creating a sparkly frame.

Start with the section of four cords on the left-hand side. String three size-11 seed beads on the outermost left strand. Next string one size-6 seed bead on to the two centre cords. Leave the fourth cord unbeaded.

15 Tie a flat knot using the outer cords (the cord with the three beads and the one with no beads) around the two inner cords (with the size-6 seed beads).

16 Repeat three times to make four sections in total. Then, on the right-hand side, tie four sections with the four cords on the right. Remember for the side sections, it is always the outer cords that hold the three seed beads, and the cords closest to the rhinestone round bead section that remain without beads.

17 Now you will create another V-shaped area of flat knots like the one on top of the roundel section. You have already tied three flat knots in a row in step 16, so the next row will be made of two flat knots. To start, use the two cords on the right side of the left-side section and the two cords from the left side of centre bead section to tie a flat knot. Then use the four cords on the right to make another flat knot. The two outermost cords on both sides will float this row.

18 For this row, separate your twelve cords into three sections of four cords each. String a 3mm crystal bead on to the two centremost cords. Tie a flat knot at the bottom of this crystal bead with one cord on either side. Then tie a flat knot to the left side of this central knot and tie a flat knot on the right side.

19 Tie two flat knots underneath this row. Remember to 'float' the first and last two cords.

20 Then, for the last row, use the central four cords to tie one flat knot.

21 Starting from the left, use the outermost cord as the filler cord for a series of six diagonal double half hitches down the left-hand side. Then use the outermost right-hand cord as the filler cord for six diagonal double half-hitch knots down the right-hand side. To secure the two sides together, use the left-hand cord as the filler cord and the right-hand cord as the wrapping cord for a final double half-hitch knot.

You have completed the first roundel of the bracelet!

22 Now create another five or six roundels, depending on the size of your wrist, and the size of the beads you've chosen. When you are finished with the last roundel section, you will start the V-shaped alternating flat knot section, but you will create an elongated version of it that will become the bed for a button.

To start, like in step 17, use the two cords on the right side of the left-side section and the two cords on the left side of centre bead section to tie a flat knot. Then use the four cords to the right of that knot to make another flat knot. The two outermost cords on both sides will float this row.

Then separate the twelve cords into three sections of four cords each and string a 3mm crystal bead on to the two centremost cords. Tie a flat knot at the bottom of this crystal bead with one cord on either side. Then tie a flat knot to the left side of this central knot and tie a flat knot on the right side.

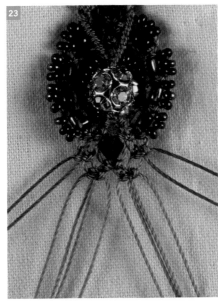

23 Tie two flat knots underneath this row. Remember to float the first and last two cords.

24 Now tie a row of three flat knots underneath the two flat knots.

25 You will be alternating rows of flat knots in a two-row, three-row sequence for 4cm (1½in). Your last row should end with one central flat knot under a two-knot row.

26 Create a line of five diagonal double half-hitch knots from the outer left-hand side that progress down to a centrepoint. Remember to use the outermost cord as the filler cord. Now do the same for the right-hand side: use the outermost right-hand cord as the filler cord for a line of five diagonal double half-hitch knots that come to the centrepoint. To tie the two sides together, use the left-hand cord as the filler cord and the right-hand cord as the wrapping cord for a final double half-hitch knot. Then create another line of diagonal double half hitches from the left, and another line from the right-hand side. Tie the two sides together with a diagonal double half-hitch knot.

27 Lock the rows of diagonal double half-hitch knots in place with a coat of clear nail polish. Wait for the polish to dry, then clip the remaining threads close to the diagonal double half hitches. Sew a button on to this buttonbed and try on your fabulous new bracelet!

Dark Side of the Moon Necklace

Muted teal, navy and black beads together present a nebulous admixture of hinted sparkles and quiet flashes of colours in the dark-sky end of the spectrum. The large bead is meant to represent the moon; the 3mm bicone bead hidden among the larger seed beads is meant to be a star. The star in this piece is barely noticeable; only you and I know it is there. You can use a seed bead instead, if you wish.

Materials

- Dark teal C-Lon cord (not C-Lon thread) 304cm (120in) lengths × 3
- Size-11 seed beads × 13
- 6mm or 8mm jet AB faceted round beads × 19
- Size-8 seed beads × 1 hank
- 3mm bicone jet beads (optional) × 19
- 10mm or 12mm dark blue or jet round crystal bead × 1
- Clear nail polish

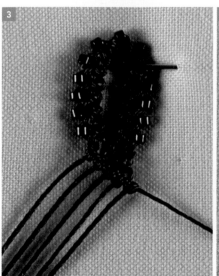

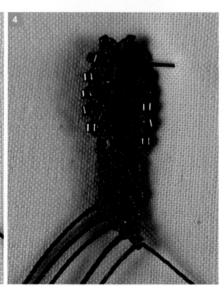

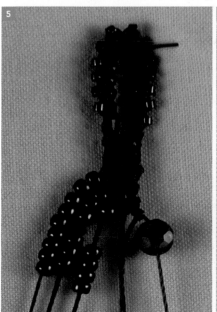

1 Create a beaded buttonhole using the directions for the **Baroque Bracelet** on page 84.

2 Tie a single flat knot on the right-hand side; do not add a seed bead here.

3 Starting from the upper left and working toward the lower right, tie a row of diagonal double half-hitch knots across the entire buttonhole.

4 Tie three more rows of diagonal double half-hitch knots.

5 String a 6mm jet AB bead on to the rightmost cord. String nine size-8 seed beads on to the leftmost cord, seven beads on to the cord next to it, and five beads on to the cord next to that. If you are going to use the 3mm bicone beads as the star, always string one as the fourth bead in the middle row of seven beads.

6 Starting from the right, tie a row of diagonal double half-hitch knots to seal in the rows of seed beads.

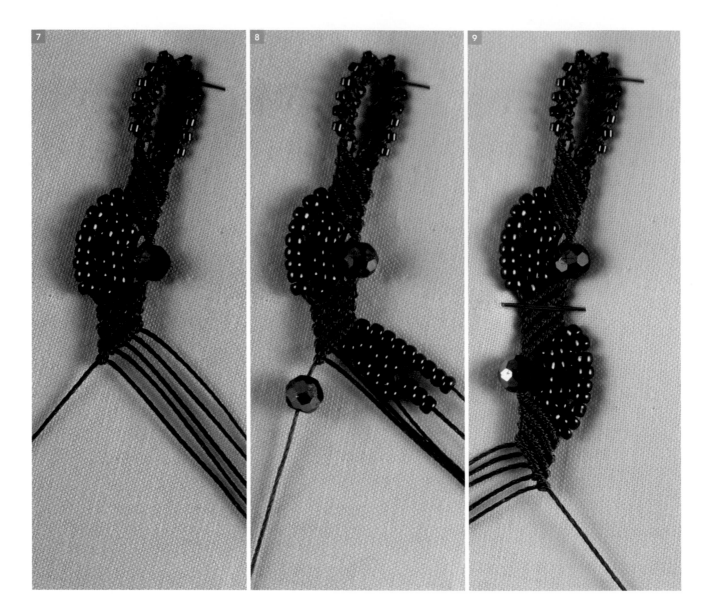

7 Tie three more rows of diagonal double half hitches below this knot.

8 String a 6mm bead on to the leftmost cord. From the right, string nine size-8 seed beads on to the rightmost cord, seven beads on to the cord to its left and five beads on to the cord next to that. As in step 5, if you are going to add a star, string the 3mm bicone bead as the fourth bead in the middle row of seven beads.

9 Tie a row of diagonal double half-hitch knots from left to right. Tie three more rows of diagonal double half-hitch knots below it. Continue this back and forth pattern until you have used all nineteen of the 6mm beads.

10 On the rightmost cord, string two size-8 seed beads. Skip a cord and string one seed bead on the third-from-right cord.

11 Use the two outer cords to tie a line of eight flat knots, enclosing the four inner cords.

12 String the 10mm or 12mm round crystal bead on to the four inner cords and tie a flat knot around it with the outside cords. With all the cords tie an overhand knot after the flat knot. Dab clear nail polish on to the knot, let it dry and clip the cords close to the knot.

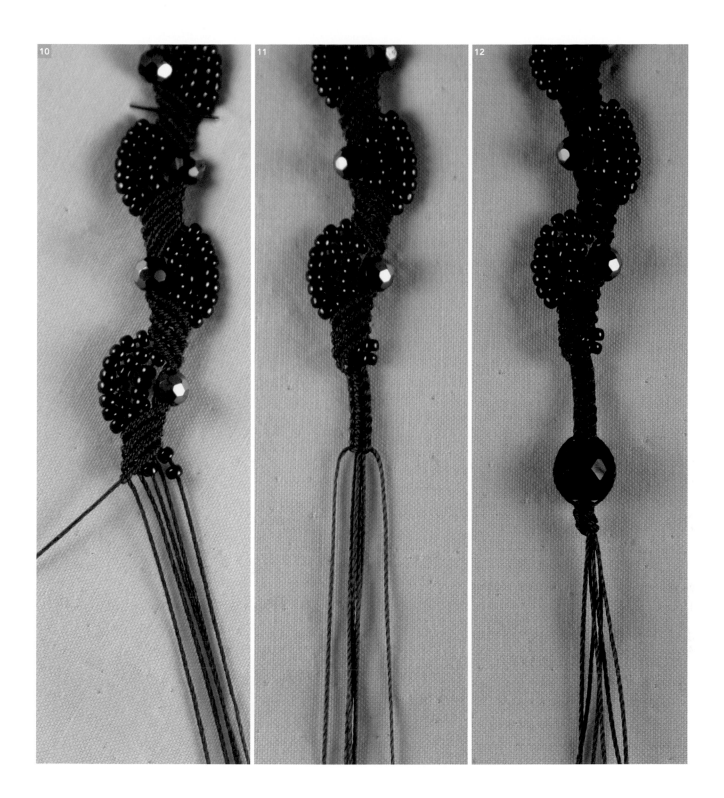

Secret Garden Bracelet

A florid bed of hot pink fuchsias. Azalea bushes bursting with springtime purples and flagrant ruby reds. Have you ever strolled into a flower garden and been overwhelmed by the joyous intensity of colour?

This bracelet features an enamelled metal slider centrepiece surrounded by crisscrosses of hot pink seed beads and sparkling petal-coloured bicones encircled by more pink beads. It is finished off by a knotted adjustable sliding closure.

Materials

- Magenta C-Lon cord (not C-Lon thread), 152cm (60in) lengths × 12
- Rectangular 12 × 18mm metal slider with a pink crystal × 1
- Red C-Lon cord (not C-Lon thread), 61cm (24in) lengths × 3
- Size-11 pink seed beads × 1 tube
- 4mm dark pink Swarovski bicone beads × 8
- 6mm pale pink Swarovski bicone beads × 4
- 4mm pink Czech fire-polished beads × 8
- Glue
- Clear nail polish

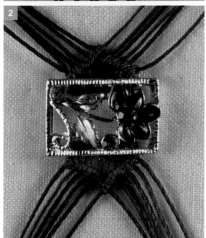

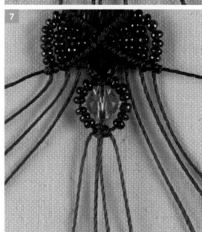

1 Fold five magenta cords in half and tie lark's head knots on to a sixth cord. Thread the sixth cord through two holes on one side of the slider and pull it tight. Do the same for the other side of the slider.

2 Turn the slider and cords over and secure the cords to a padded clipboard. Tie a diagonal double half-hitch row using the outermost cords as the filler cords and working toward the centre.

3 String seven seed beads on the outermost left cord, five seed beads on the cord next to it, three seed beads on the cord next to that one and one bead on the fourth cord. Do the same for the right side.

4 Using the sixth cord in from the right as the filler cord, tie a row of diagonal double half-hitch knots outward and to the right.

5 Then repeat on the left side creating an inverted V under the seed beads.

6 String a 4mm bicone bead on the two inner cords and enclose it in a flat knot using the two cords on the sides of the inner cords.

7 Beneath the 4mm bead, string a pale pink 6mm bicone bead on the two inner cords. String six seed beads on its side cords and tie a flat knot under the bicone bead.

8 String another 4mm bicone bead under the pale pink bead on the two inner cords and tie it in a flat knot with its side cords.

9 Now we'll focus on the four outer cords on the left and right sides. Starting from the interior, tie two outward-bound rows of diagonal double half-hitch knots on the left and right sides. String three seed beads on the innermost of the cords, skip a cord, and string one seed bead on the second from outermost cords.

10 Tie two rows of diagonal double half-hitch knots going from the outermost cords toward the interior.

11 Tie a row of diagonal double half-hitch knots incorporating all the cords and ending in the centre under the 4mm bead.

12 Repeat steps 3–11 so that you have two complete sequences.

13 String a seed bead on the second cord from the left side and fourth cord from the left side. Do the same for the right side. String a 4mm pink fire-polished bead on to the middle two cords.

14 Starting from the left-hand side, tie a row of diagonal double half-hitch knots that slant down toward the centre point. Then tie a row of diagonal double half hitches from the right-hand side. Add an additional row of diagonal double half-hitch knots on the left-hand side and another on the right-hand side.

15 String a seed bead on the second and fourth cords on both sides.

16 Tie two rows of diagonal double half hitches below them using the outermost cords as the filler cords and working toward the centre. Repeat step 15, then tie three rows of diagonal double half-hitch knots using the outermost cords as the filler cords and working toward the centre. Trim the three outer cords on each side, leaving six cords hanging down.

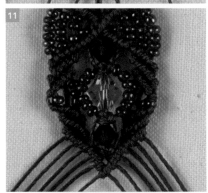

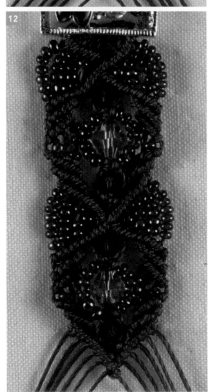

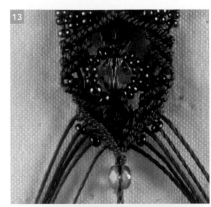

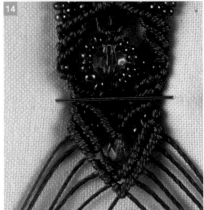

17 Repeat steps 3–16 on the other side of the metal slider. When the second band is complete, cross the loose cords over each other. Use the three strands of red cord to tie a huge flat knot around the twelve magenta cords, pulling the flat knots very tight.

18 Tie three more flat knots with the red cords. Coat the outside of the flat knots with clear glue to seal the knots together. Try to avoid getting any glue on the twelve magenta cords. Clip the red cords close to the flat knots. Use either clear glue or clear nail polish to seal the knots. After they're dry to the touch, clip the red cords close to the knots.

19 The final step to this pretty bracelet is to string a single 4mm pink fire-polished bead on to the twelve hanging magenta cords, using one bead every two cords. Tie the cords about 2.5cm (1in) away from the flat knot closure with overhand knots. Seal the knots with clear nail polish and clip the cords close to the knots when the polish is dry.

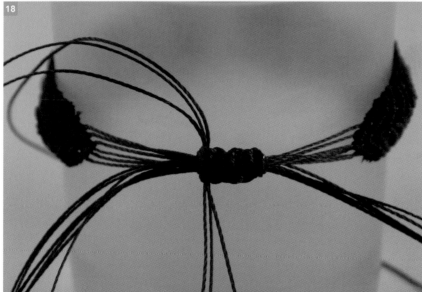

Stained Glass Bracelet

An assortment of 6mm crystal beads framed in black cord and seed beads gives this bracelet the semblance of a stained glass panel tucked away in a quiet corner of an abbey or church. Make this little slice of heaven with the leftovers from your other beading projects. It requires twelve 6mm beads of differing colours and forty-eight size 4mm fire-polished or bicone crystal glass beads.

I break this bracelet down into twelve segments of five beads each: a central section of one 6mm bead flanked by four size 4mm beads, two on each side.

Materials

- Black Tuff Cord no. 3, 152cm (60in) lengths × 6
- 6mm crystal glass beads, an assortment of colours and shapes × 12
- Size-11 black seed beads
- 4mm crystal glass beads × 48
- Button
- Sewing thread and needle
- Clear nail polish

1   Lay out your assortment of beads to create a pattern harmonious to your own sense of aesthetics. Mix and match them as you please!

Moonbeam Bracelet

Like many of the other pieces in this book, this Moonbeam Bracelet is modular; it features five roundels of diamonds made of opposing rows of diagonal double half hitches and moon beads enclosed by lacy flat knots, surrounded by a buttonhole and a buttonbed. The diamond-shaped curtains of macramé cord that frame the luminescent periwinkle AB fire-polished beads above and below the cheery full moon faces are created using the same technique that's in the Paristan Necklace.

Let this happy-go-lucky bracelet brighten your disposition with its lineup of celestial charms. What's not to love?

Materials

- Purple Tuff Cord no. 3, 152cm (60in) lengths × 6
- Size-11 lavender Delica seed beads × ½ tube
- 5mm periwinkle AB fire-polished beads × 6
- Silver-tone moon beads × 6
- Size-8 lavender seed beads × ½ tube
- 3mm periwinkle AB beads × 40
- Clear nail polish

1   Create a beaded buttonhole of sixteen flat knots using the directions for the **Baroque Bracelet** on page 84.

2   Create the roundels. Tie the two sides of the buttonhole together with a flat knot made up of the two innermost cords from the left side and the two innermost cords from the right side.

3   Tie a flat knot with the outermost four cords from the left and the outermost four cords from the right.

4   Using the sixth cord in from the right as the holding cord, tie a row of five diagonal double half hitches to the right.

5   Do the same for the left side, using the sixth cord in from the left as the holding cord.

6   To create the diamond-shaped frame, you'll create a row of diagonal double half hitches by knotting the wrapping cords in reverse order. Tie the fourth cord from the left on to the holding cord (the outermost cord) with a diagonal double half-hitch knot. Then tie the third-from-the-left cord on to the holding cord, then the second from the left, and finally the first cord on the left. Make sure to align the knots so that they create an upside-down V shape.

On the right side, use the fourth cord from the right as the first wrapping cord and use the rightmost cord as the holding cord, the third from the right as the second wrapping cord, the second as the third wrapping cord, and the first as the last wrapping cord in a row of diagonal double half hitches. The two centre cords are reserved for stringing the 5mm bead on to.

7   Thread a 5mm bead on to the two inner cords. Use those inner cords to tie two diagonal double half-hitch knots by tying the left inner cord to the left-hand row of diagonal double half hitches, then tying the right-hand cord to the right-hand row of diagonal double half hitches. This will bring the left- and right-hand rows of cords together to a point below the 5mm bead.

8   Finish the point by tying the two filler cords together using the left cord as the filler cord and the right cord as the wrapping cord for a final double half-hitch knot.

9 Thread a moon bead on to the two centre cords. On the cords on either side of it string seven size-11 seed beads on to each cord and tie a flat knot under the moon bead.

10 For the four outer cords to the left of the moon section, string two size-8 seed beads on to the outer cord and one 3mm AB bead on to the second cord. Leave the third cord without beads. Tie a flat knot under the 3mm bead.

11 Do three more of these sequences on the left side.

12 Now make four sequences on the right side.

13 Tie a row of diagonal double half hitches starting from the centre (follow steps 4–6 to make the diamond window frame on the other side of the moon bead). You've completed one roundel.

14 This bracelet takes five roundels to be long enough to encompass a wrist, so build four more roundels.

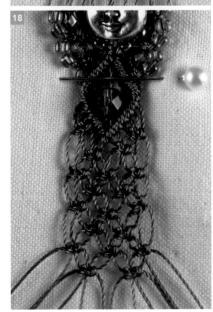

15 Create the buttonbed. After the fifth roundel is knotted, make one final diamond frame under the moon bead. Add a flat knot below each side of the diamond frame by using the outer four cords on the left side for the first flat knot and the outer four cords on the right for the second flat knot.

16 Tie two flat knots below that using the innermost four cords on each side for each knot.

17 Now tie a row of three flat knots using four cords apiece.

18 Tie a row of two knots, followed by a row of three knots, a row of two knots, a row of three knots, and finish up with a row of two knots.

19 Tie a single flat knot with the four centre cords.

20 Create two rows of diagonal double half-hitch knots, ending in the centre.

21 Flip the bracelet over, dab clear nail polish on the last row of diagonal double half-hitch knots, and wait for the polish to dry. Trim the cords close to the last row of knots. Sew a button on to the buttonbed or fashion a button out of a moon bead and add it to the buttonbed.

Starry Starry Night Ornament

Holiday ornament or sun catcher, this five-pointed star pays homage to icy, clear, starry winter skies. If knotted correctly, the sides won't wilt or droop, so it is ideal for dressing a Christmas tree or adding a festive touch to a frosty window. Once you are comfortable making this star, consider experimenting with six-pointed or even seven-pointed stars; just add four cords per point.

I adore the tiny rhinestone wrecking ball at the centre of the star; it's a cosmic snowball with sparkle aplenty!

Materials

- Pale turquoise BeadSmith no. 6 or turquoise Stringth no. 3, 76cm (30in) lengths × 20
- 8mm or 10mm silver-plated rhinestone round, with either peridot or green rhinestones × 1
- 8mm pale blue Swarovski bicone beads × 5
- Size-11 seed beads in a sparkly pastel blue or green × 1 tube
- 6mm pale green Swarovski bicone beads × 5
- 4mm pale blue Swarovski bicone beads × 5
- 6mm pale blue Swarovski bicone beads × 5
- 4mm pale green Swarovski bicone beads × 5
- Clear nail polish

1 String both ends of one of the cords through the rhinestone round bead leaving about 2.5cm (1in) of looped cord at the top of the rhinestone bead. Tie nine lark's head knots on to the cord to the right of the bead and ten lark's head knots on to the cord to the left of the bead.

2 Thread the ends of the cords back to front through the loop at the top of the rhinestone round bead.

3 Draw the cords as tight as you can and tie the two cords into a full knot.

4 Divide the lark's head knots into five sections.

5 On one section tie two rows of diagonal double half-hitch knots starting from the outer cords and knotting to the centre cords.

6 Repeat on all the sections.

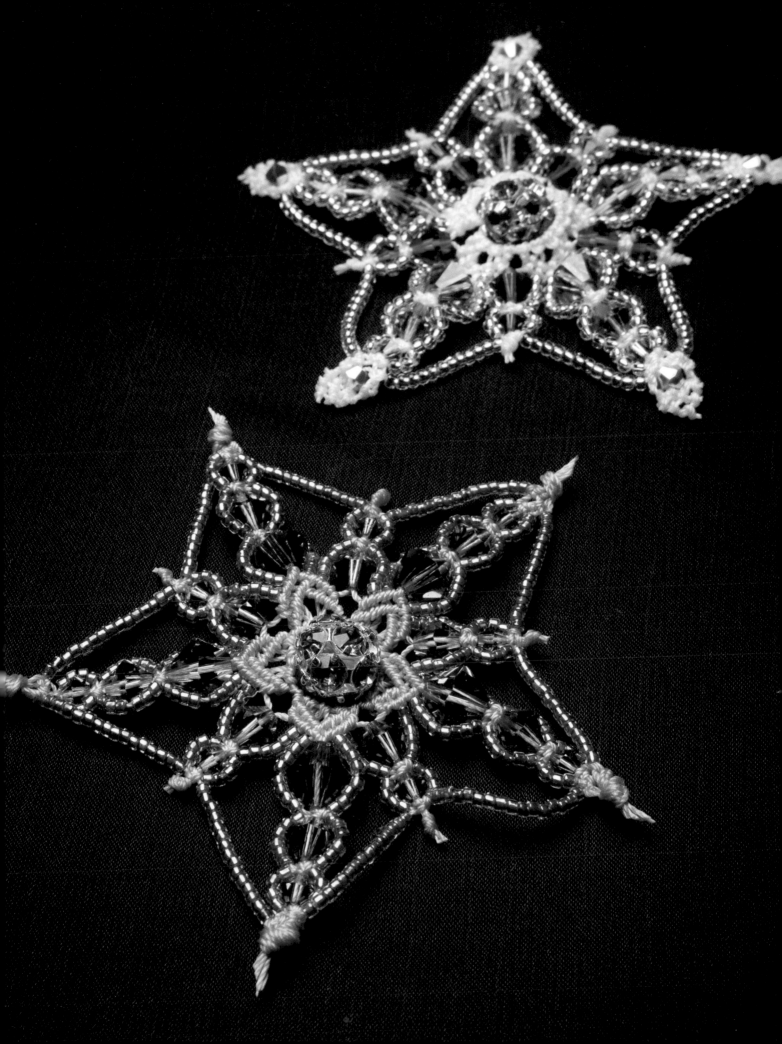

7 These instructions will be the same for all five sections. Thread a pale blue 8mm bicone bead on to the two centre cords.

8 String eight seed beads on to the cords adjacent to the two centre cords and tie a full knot, enclosing the 8mm bead.

9 Follow this by stringing a pale green 6mm bicone bead on to the two centre cords, and six seed beads on each cord next to the centre cords. Tie a full knot.

10 Now string a pale blue 4mm bead on to the two centre cords, and four seed beads on to its neighbour cords, and tie a full knot.

11 Starting with the 8mm bicone bead, complete all five sections.

12 These instructions will be the same for all five side sections. Take the outermost cords from two sections and string a pale blue 6mm bicone bead on to it.

13 String six seed beads on to the cords on either side of the centre cords and tie a full knot with them enclosing the 6mm bead.

14 Now string a pale green 4mm bicone bead on to the two centre cords and four seed beads on the cords surrounding them and tie a full knot.

15 These directions apply to all five points of the star. Take the two outer cords from this section made in the previous steps and string fifteen seed beads on to each of them. Depending on the type of seed bead used, you may need sixteen or fourteen seed beads instead. Using a flat knot, tie each outer cord to the closest two cords on the main points of the star.

16 Tie all five points together in this manner.

17 Tie each star point with an overhand knot. Tie the two cords on each side section with an overhand knot. Seal all the knots with clear nail polish. When dry, clip close to the overhand knots. Keep the cords on one of the star points long enough to serve as a hanging loop.

Great heavenly days! You're finished.

Mariposa Necklace

Inspired by the delicacy of a butterfly's wings, Mariposa is comprised of teardrop-shaped AB fire-polished Czech beads and seed beads in two sizes: size-11 beads encompass iridescent size-8 beads, forming sparkling lace around the central crystals.

Four types of knots are used: lark's heads, diagonal double half hitches, overhands and flat knots.

The trickiest part is getting the tension right when looping the thread through the butterfly body and tying the knot to form the head; it's a matter of adjusting the looped thread carefully as the knot is being tied. You can leave the antennae intact, bead them or cut them to suit your taste.

Materials

- Medium blue Tuff Cord no. 3, 380cm (150in) lengths × 9
- Purple Tuff Cord no. 3, 380cm (150in) lengths × 9
- Black Tuff Cord no. 3, 46cm (18in) length × 1
- 19mm black oblong pressed-glass bead × 1
- Size-8 purple iridescent seed beads × 1 tube
- 4mm lilac Swarovski faceted round beads × 2
- 10mm AB blue teardrop crystal beads × 4
- Size-11 transparent rainbow periwinkle AB blue seed beads × 1 hank
- Size-11 dark blue iridescent seed beads × ¼ tube (optional)
- 6mm dark sapphire Swarovski bicone beads × 2
- 4mm medium blue Czech fire-polished beads × 1 strand
- 10mm pale blue round fire-polished bead × 1
- Clear nail polish

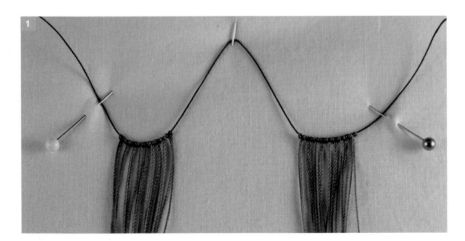

1 Alternating the purple and blue cords, tie two sets of nine lark's head knots on to the black cord.

2 Thread the black cord through the oblong pressed-glass bead and draw the two sets of lark's head knots closer together. Leave about 5–8cm (2–3in) of looped cord at the top of the oblong bead.

3 Wrap the ends of the black cord around the loop at the top of the pressed-glass bead and tie an overhand knot. Crop the ends of the black cord to form antennae.

Separate the coloured cords into four sections: the top left and top right sections will have five lark's head knots; the lower two sides will each hold four lark's head knots.

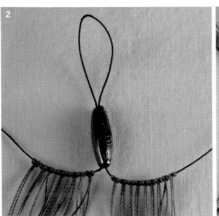

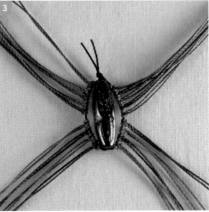

Mermaid's Trove Necklace

A mermaid's trove is a collection of the bits and bobs from shipwrecks that filter down to the sandy bottom of the sea. The mermaids who dwell in the deep pluck these shiny baubles out of the sand and knot them into their jewellery.

This triangular necklace has three similar segments that are finished differently. The segment that hangs down in the centre is tipped by a teardrop crystal bead. The other two form the arms that wrap around your neck and close at the nape.

If you have the patience and skill to ream out the tiny holes in freshwater pearls, use them in this neckpiece instead of the three size 8mm bicone beads.

Materials

- Medium blue Tuff Cord no. 3 or blue Stringth no. 3, 380cm (150in) lengths × 18
- 10mm Czech, Chinese or Austrian crystal glass beads × 2
- 8mm Swarovski bicone beads or reamed freshwater pearls × 3
- Size-11 iridescent teal seed beads × 1 box
- 4mm fire-polished crystal beads × 46
- Size-8 iridescent teal seed beads × 1 tube
- 10 × 6mm teal teardrop crystal bead × 1
- Clear nail polish

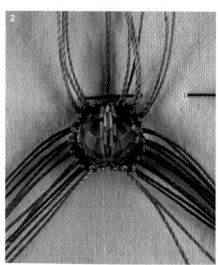

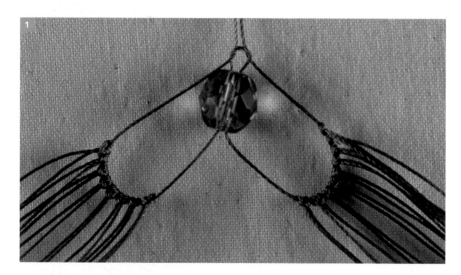

1 Fold one of the cords in half and loop it through the 10mm centre bead. Leave about 2.5cm (1in) of looped cord at the top of the bead. Tie eight lark's head knots on one side of the cord and nine lark's head knots on the other side. String the ends of the holding cord through the loop at the top of the centre bead.

2 Pull the cords as tight as you can. Tie a flat knot with these two cords.

Separate the lark's head knots into three sections of six knots each. The flat knot used to secure the cords to the bead should be in the middle of one of the sections.

3 Create three V-shaped sets of diagonal double half-hitch knots. For each set, use the outermost cords as the filler cords as you create a slanting line of diagonal double half hitches that come to a point in the centre. For the final knot that ties the two sides together at the point, wrap the right-hand filler cord over the left-hand filler cord in a double half-hitch knot.

17 Separate the two outermost cords from each side and either pin or tape them out of the way. With the remaining cords, tie a row of diagonal double half hitches, ending in the centre.

18 Separate the outermost cords on both sides and pin or tape aside. Create another row of diagonal double half-hitch knots with the six remaining cords.

19 Trim all the loose cords on this segment except for the innermost two. String the teardrop bead on to these cords and secure it to the necklace with an overhand knot.

You have now finished knotting the portion that hangs down in the middle. Knot both of the other portions of the necklace to this point; omit adding the teardrop bead and clipping the loose cords.

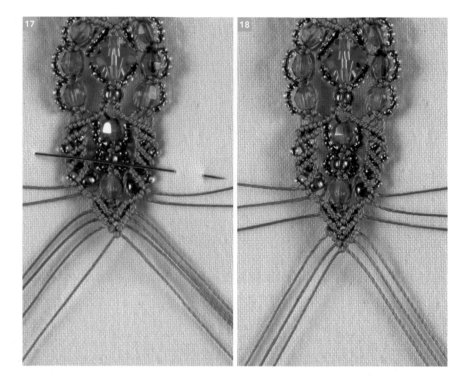

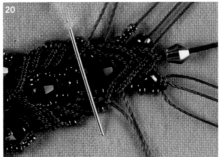

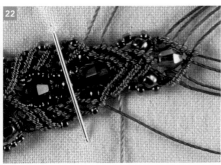

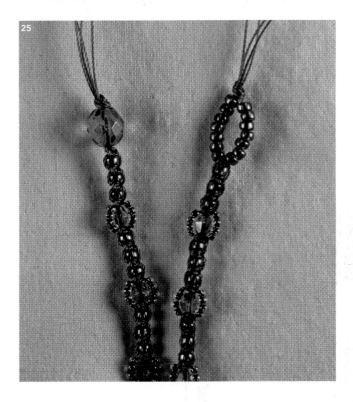

20 Now it's time to complete the arms of the necklace. On the right portion, separate the two outermost cords on each side and tape or pin them out of the way. There should be eight cords remaining. On the outermost of the eight remaining cords, thread three size-11 seed beads. On the inner cords next to them string one size-8 seed bead. Skip a cord and string a 4mm bead on to the two centre cords.

21 Tie a flat knot under the size-8 seed bead cords using the cords adjacent to them.

22 Tie a row of diagonal double half-hitch knots starting from the outermost cords and ending in a point under the 4mm bead.

23 Tie two more rows of diagonal double half hitches. Repeat this sequence twice more.

24 Separate the two outermost cords on each side and pin or tape them out of the way. String a 4mm bead on the two inner cords. String four size-11 seed beads on the side cords and use them to tie a flat knot below the 4mm bead. String a size-8 seed bead on the inner cords and secure it with a flat knot. Knot two more size-8 seed beads the same way, then add a 4mm bead with four seed beads on the outer cords and tie a flat knot. Continue this pattern for 13.5mm (5¼in).

25 Follow steps 20–24 to complete the left arm of the necklace.

Finish the ends of the necklace by stringing a 10mm bead on one set of cords and securing it with an overhand knot. For the other end of the necklace, divide the four remaining cords into two and string seven size-11 beads on one set and seven beads on to the other set. Tie them together with an overhand knot.

Dab all knots next to loose cords with clear nail polish. After the polish is dry, clip all the loose cords.

Leaf Choker

My inspiration for this choker is a Chinese scarf that has sinuous silver threads sandwiched between two layers of gossamer silk. The thread floats shift patterns every time the scarf moves. I've tried to recreate that lyrical effect with this micro-macramé choker. The leaf bracelet is a companion piece. Both use only two types of macramé knots: the double half hitch and the flat knot.

The micro-macramé leaf shapes are formed by enclosing seed beads between two arced rows of diagonal double half hitches. Adding seed beads inside the leaf motifs gives this pattern a shimmery stained glass look. The floating cords surrounding the leaves lend an airy, delicate feel to these pieces.

Materials

- 2 × 1.25cm (¾ × ⁹/₁₆in) Balinese carved bone face × 1
- 4cm (1½in) square scraps of ultrasuede × 2
- Size-11 seed beads in complementary assorted colours × 1 hank
- Nymo B beading thread
- Size-12 beading needle
- Adhesive tape, 5cm (2in) length × 1
- Medium blue Tuff Cord no. 3 or blue BeadSmith 'no stretch' no. 6, 203cm (80in) lengths × 16
- Pewter flower button × 1
- Clear glue
- Clear nail polish

1 Prepare the cabochon. Glue the bone face on to the ultrasuede backing.

2 Add the seed beads around the cabochon by stringing several beads on to a threaded beading needle and sewing them into the ultrasuede around the bone face (see page 9).

3 Carefully cut away the excess ultrasuede around the beads, making sure you don't cut into the thread inside the beads.

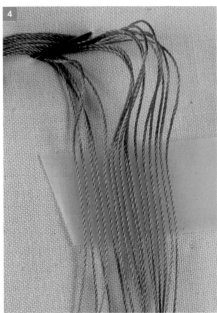

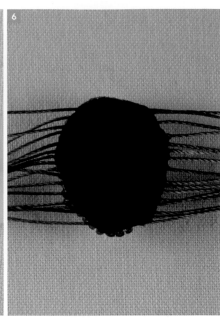

4 Measure 101.5cm (40in) into the cords and make note of this point; this is where the cabochon will be placed. Put a piece of adhesive tape, sticky side up, on the padded clipboard. Arrange and stick the sixteen cords on top of the tape.

5 Add a line of glue to all of the cords and place the beaded bone face on top of the glue.

6 When the glue is dry, peel the adhesive tape off the cords. Turn the cabochon over and glue another piece of ultrasuede, cut to the same size as the cabochon, over the back of the cords.

7 Anchor the cords on the side of the choker that you're not working on. Twist those strands of cords not in use around long straight pins pinned into the padded clipboard. Don't be afraid to use lots of straight pins – it is important to keep the cabochon stabilised and flat on the board. This helps to keep your knots consistent.

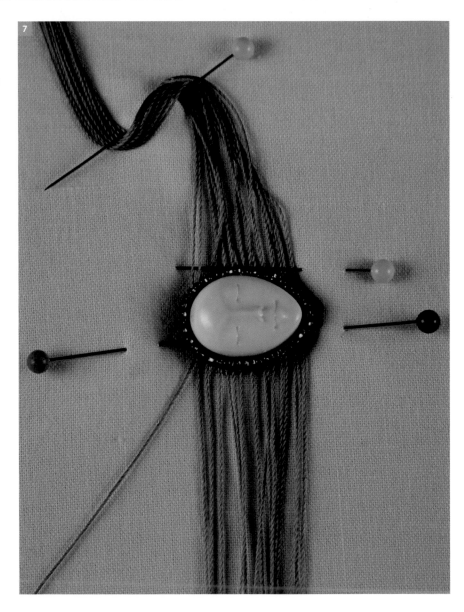

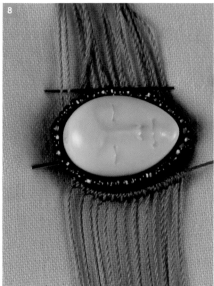

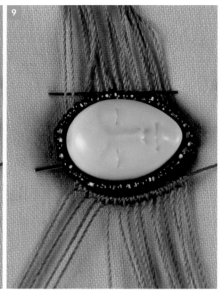

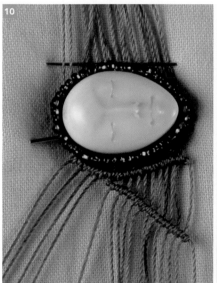

8 Tie a line of double half hitches around the bone face – this frames the face and creates even spaces between the threads.

9 Separate the threads into two sections – one section will have the four threads you won't be using for this leaf. The fifth thread in from the left is the starting thread for the leaf pattern.

10 Tie a row of diagonal double half-hitch knots using the fifth cord from the left as the holding cord. It isn't necessary to shape this row of diagonal double half hitches into an arc as you work it; adding the second row of diagonal double half hitches to enclose the seed beads will cause the cords to mould around the seed beads, forming a leaf.

11 After completing the row of diagonal double half hitches, add one seed bead to the seventh cord from the left, add two seed beads to the ninth cord, three seed beads to the eleventh cord, two seed beads to the thirteenth cord and one seed bead to the fifteenth cord.

12 Now work a second row of diagonal double half-hitch knots around the seed beads. Start with the fifth cord in from the left, and use the beads to guide the knots as you work this row. Your first leaf is done.

13 Now the fifth strand from the right becomes the new starting point for the next leaf. Tie a row of diagonal double half-hitch knots using the fifth cord from the right as the holding cord.

14 String one seed bead on to the cord second from the left, two beads on to the fourth cord, three beads on to the sixth cord, two beads on to the eighth cord and one bead on to the tenth cord.

15 Enclose them with a row of diagonal double half-hitch knots using the fifth cord from the right as the filler cord.

16 Create another sixteen leaves in this fashion until you have a length about half the diameter of your neck. Tie a horizontal row of double half-hitch knots using the leftmost cord as the filler cord and working straight across from left to right to finish the leaf portion of this side of the neckpiece. Try to make this row as straight as possible.

17 Create a bed of alternating flat knots for the button to be sewn into. Tie four flat knots across the piece. Under them tie three flat knots, leaving off the outer two cords on each side.

18 Follow this with a row of four flat knots, followed by a row of three flat knots. Follow this pattern two more times, then tie two flat knots with the eight centre cords, and finally one flat knot with the innermost four cords.

19 Add two rows of diagonal double half hitches using the outermost cords as the filler cords and working toward the centre.

20 Now build the other half of the choker. When you've completed nineteen leaves, tie a row of horizontal double half-hitch knots across the piece using the leftmost cord as the filler cord and working from left to right. Separate the outer two cords from both sides and either tie or pin them out of the way. Create another line of horizontal double half-hitch knots using the leftmost cord of the remaining twelve cords as the filler cord and working from left to right.

21 Separate two more cords from each side and tape or pin them aside. Create two lines of seven flat knots with seed beads separating each knot.

22 Tie a flat knot using the inner two cords from the left side and the two inner cords from the right side.

23 Tie two rows of diagonal double half-hitch knots using the outermost cords as the filler cords and working toward the centre.

Seal the last row of knots with a dab of clear nail polish. Seal all the other knots next to loose cords on the choker. Wait for the polish to dry, then clip all the loose cords. Sew the flower button on to the buttonbed.

Leaf Bracelet

A few years ago I was browsing through a used book shop and came across a macramé pamphlet from the 1970s that featured an entire curtain of cascading macramé leaves. Imagine my chagrin when I returned home, pamphlet in hand, and discovered that the leaf pattern wasn't even in the instructions – so I had to invent my own! I added beads to the centre of my leaves to punch a little extra colour into them.

This bracelet contains the same leaf motifs as the choker in the previous project, but building the bracelet progresses in a different manner. While the buttonhole for the choker is the finishing touch, the buttonhole for the bracelet is the beginning sequence.

Materials

- Medium blue Tuff Cord no. 3 or blue BeadSmith 'no stretch' no. 6, 152cm (60in) lengths × 6
- Size-11 seed beads in complimentary assorted colours × ½ hank
- Pewter flower button × 1
- Needle and thread
- Clear nail polish

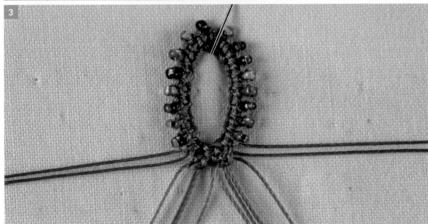

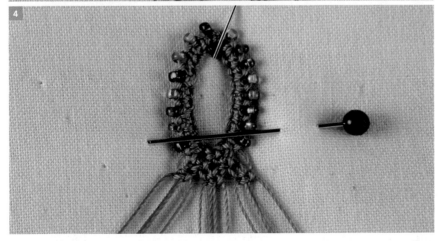

1 Use all six cords to create a buttonhole using the directions for the **Baroque Bracelet** (see page 84).

2 Take the two innermost threads from both sides and tie a flat knot to close the buttonhole.

3 Tie two flat knots under this central flat knot using the inner four cords from the left side for one knot and the inner four cords from the right side for the other knot.

4 Now tie three flat knots below them.

5 Tie a row of double half-hitch knots straight across the piece using the leftmost cord as the filler cord and working from left to right. This is to even the playing field of cords.

6 Separate the threads into two sections – one section will have the four threads you won't be using for this leaf. The fifth thread in from the left is the starting thread for the leaf pattern. Create a row of diagonal double half-hitch knots using this strand as the holding cord; the next seven cords will wrap around this cord as you create the diagonal double half-hitch knots. It is not necessary to try to shape the line of first diagonal double half hitches into an arc as you work it; after the beads are in place, adding the second line of diagonal double half hitches causes the cords to mould around the seed beads, making a leaf shape.

7 After completing the row of seven diagonal double half hitches, add seed beads to some of the seven cords: strand three gets one bead, strand five gets two beads, and strand seven gets one bead.

8 Now work the second row of diagonal double half-hitch knots. Start again with the fifth cord in from the left as the holding cord, and draw the cords tightly around the beads as you work this row.

9 Now the fifth cord from the right becomes the new holding cord for the next leaf.

Starting here, tie a row of diagonal half hitches. String one seed bead on to the seventh cord from the right, string two beads on to the ninth cord and one bead on to the eleventh cord.

10 Enclose them in a row of diagonal double half hitches using the fifth cord from the right as the holding cord.

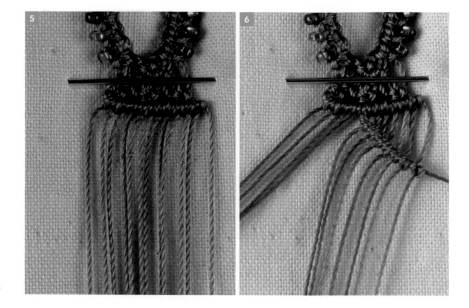

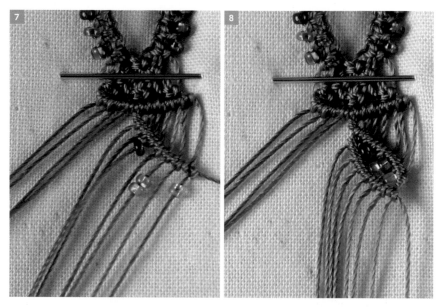

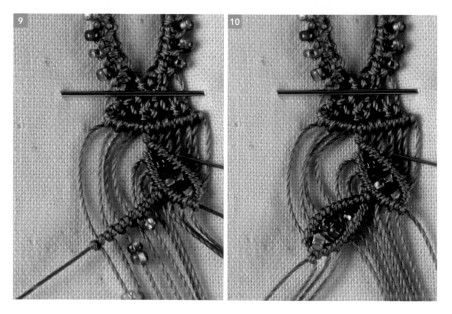

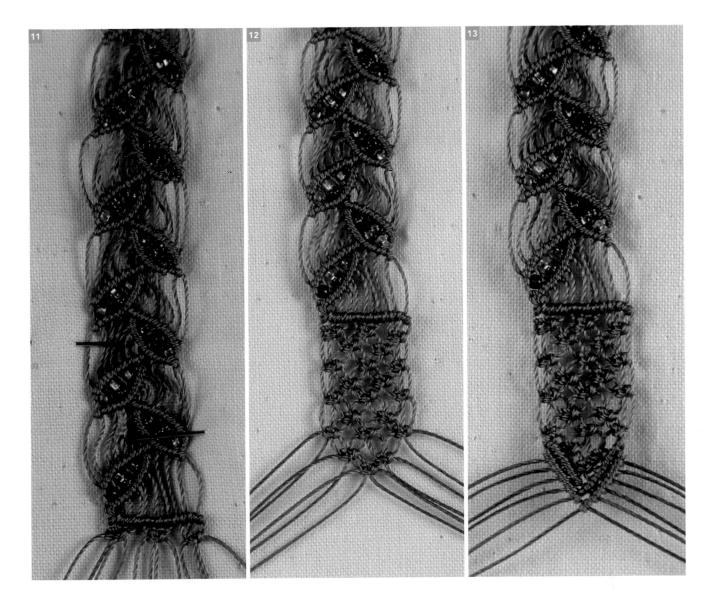

11 Create twelve or fourteen or so of the leaf shapes until you have a length about the diameter of your wrist. Don't worry too much about getting the leaves perfectly even; consistency will come as you work your way through the piece. Finish the leaf section by creating a row of double half-hitch knots straight across the piece using the leftmost cord as the filler cord and working from left to right. Add three flat knots under the line of double half-hitch knots.

12 Next you'll create a bed of alternating flat knots for the button to be sewn into. The pattern is as follows:

two flat knots
three flat knots
two flat knots
three flat knots
two flat knots
three flat knots
two flat knots
one flat knot in the centre

13 Now tie two rows of diagonal double half-hitch knots using the outermost cords as the filler cords and working toward the centre.

Lock the knots in place with clear nail polish, wait for the nail polish to dry and crop the remaining threads as close as possible to the knots.

Sew your fancy button on to this buttonbed and try on your new bracelet!

Victoriana Bracelet

A celebration of deep red crystal dotted with golden seed beads, this sweet bracelet harks back to the garnet jewellery so popular in Victorian times. It isn't as difficult as it looks – it's constructed by weaving lines of knotted beads back into a base of large bicone crystals. Find an exquisite antique button to add that finishing touch.

Materials

- Burgundy Tuff Cord no. 3, 380cm (150in) lengths × 3
- Size-8 gold/violet/green MR seed beads × 1 tube
- 8mm padparadscha volcano Swarovski bicone beads × 3
- Antiqued 1.5cm (⅝in) brass button × 1
- Size-11 metallic light bronze IR Miyuki Delica beads × 1 box
- Size-11 black seed beads × 1 tube
- Clear nail polish

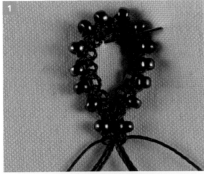

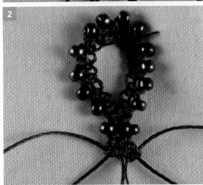

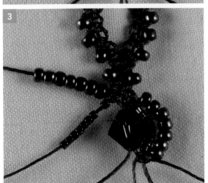

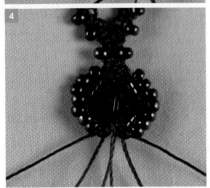

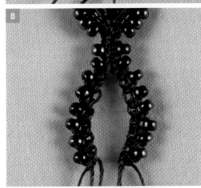

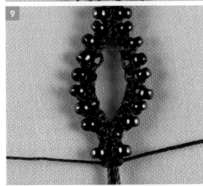

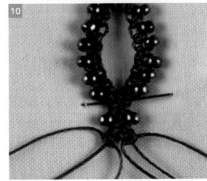

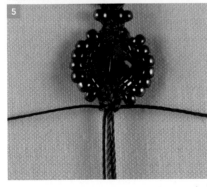

1. Create a buttonhole by tying twelve flat knots, enclosing one cord inside the knot and including a size-8 seed bead on one side of the tying cord of each knot as on the **Baroque Bracelet** (see page 84). Close the buttonhole with a flat knot using the outermost two cords to enclose the other four cords. String a size-8 seed bead on both outer cords and tie a flat knot below them.

2. Separate the cords from the two sides and tie two flat knots.

3. String an 8mm bicone bead on to the two inner cords. String eight Delica seed beads on the cords to the sides of the 8mm bicone bead. String seven size-8 seed beads on to the outer cords of each side.

4. Tie two flat knots below the 8mm bicone bead using three cords for each flat knot.

5. Tie a single flat knot under these two knots using the outer cords on both sides to enclose the inner four cords.

6. String a size-8 seed bead on to each of the outer cords and tie a flat knot.

7. Split the cords into two sections. Create a line of seven flat knots flanked by size-8 seed beads between each knot on the right.

8. Repeat the same on the left.

9. Tie all the cords together into one flat knot. String a size-8 seed bead on to each of the outer cords and tie a flat knot.

10. Tie two flat knots below it as in step 4.

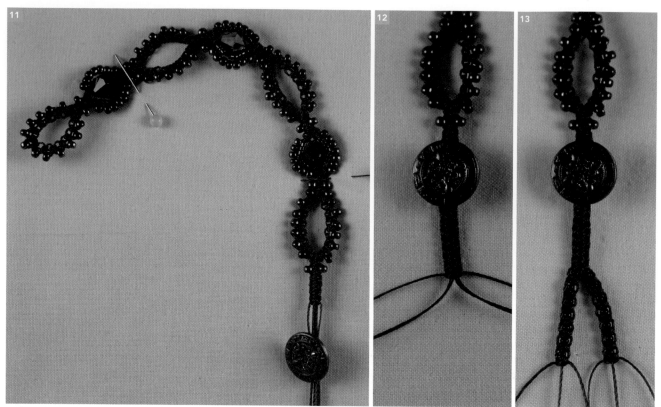

11 Repeat steps 3–10 two more times until you have three sections. Tie four more flat knots and string the button on to all of the cords.

12 Tie ten more flat knots after the button.

13 Split the six cords into two sections. String a size-11 black cherry seed bead on to the middle cord in each three-cord section and tie a flat knot around it. Tie another seven knots this way down each side.

14 Flip the piece over and thread the two sides through the opening below the button in the bracelet.

15 Bring the two sides of seed beads to the front of the piece and tie around four central cords using a flat knot.

16 Repeat steps 13–15, except threading it through the next opening.

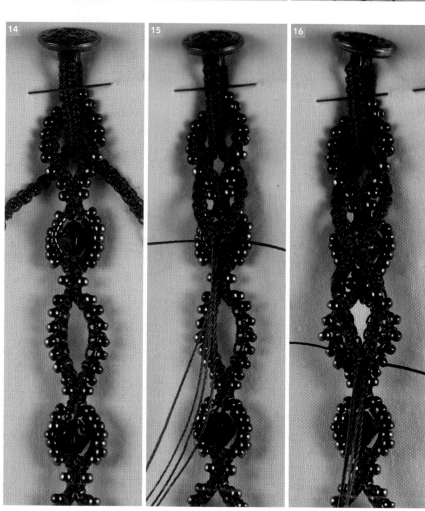

17 Split the six cords into two sections. On each section string a size-8 seed bead on to the outer cord and a size-11 black cherry seed bead on to the inner cord. Tie a flat knot. Repeat this eleven times.

18 Repeat on the right side. The combination of these two sections will serve as an outer frame around an 8mm bicone bead.

19 Combine all six cords in one flat knot.

20 Repeat steps 13–16, creating two interwoven sections as before.

21 Separate the six cords into two sections. Tie two flat knots, one on each side, then thread a black cherry seed bead on the central cords of each flat knot and enclose each bead with another flat knot. Do this five more times for a total of six beads enclosed by flat knots on each line.

22 Finish the bracelet by tying a flat knot to close the two sides together using only the four inner cords. Tie two lines of diagonal double half-hitch knots with all six cords.

Dab clear nail polish on the last row of diagonal double half-hitch knots. Wait for the polish to dry, then clip the six cords close to the knots.

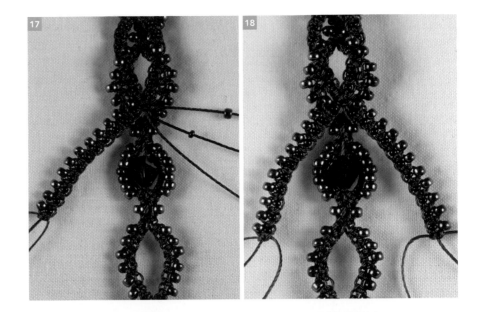

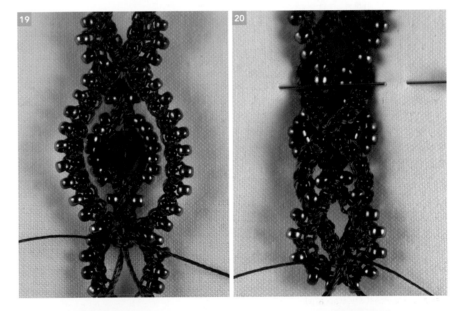

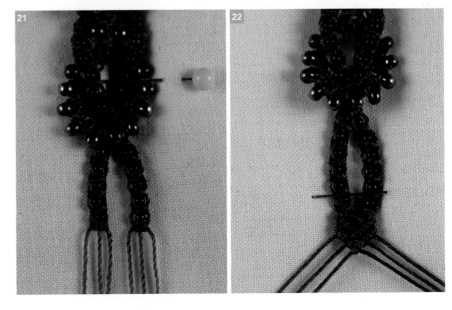

Tips

- Cut cord tips at an angle for easier threading.

- Fray Check on a cord tip will stiffen it so that beads can be more easily strung on to the cord.

- Iron unruly cords on your iron's lowest setting. Draw the threads between the ironing board and the iron placed hot-side down on the ironing board.

- Use lots of pins to hold pieces in place and stabilise them, especially when you're working on diagonal double half hitches. This will aid in the overall consistency and shape of your piece in progress.

- You can also use Scotch tape to stabilise threads, and hold newly glued pieces in place as the glue sets.

- Use a lit stick of incense instead of a candle flame for melting nylon cord ends.

- Use clear nail polish to seal lighter-coloured pieces; use a singeing device for darker pieces.

- When you go shopping for beads, take a piece of the micro-macramé cord that you'll use with you to see if the beads you want to use actually fit over the cord and how much leeway there is between the diameter of the hole and the cord.

- If you are unsure of a new knotting technique, do a sample first.

- Nylon cording is more user-friendly than cotton embroidery floss and silk cording when it comes to removing knotting mistakes.

- Use a pin or sewing needle to loosen knot mistakes.

- Use long quilting pins with plastic pinheads to stabilise your work. They're easier to grasp and their shanks are longer.

- Salvage the buckles from your old watchstraps and usable findings from necklaces and bracelets, such as lobster clasps and O-rings.

- Use a dental floss threader to thread cord in tight places, like on to a watchstrap spring bar. You can also use a length of small-gauge wire as a large-eyed needle for the same purpose by folding the wire in half and twisting the ends together loosely. Thread your cord through the eye created in the wire.

- Pearls, although their holes are small, can be reamed out with graduated hand reamers or with a Dremel tool or flexible shaft tool.

- If you are working on a project that requires several long pieces of cord but you've run short of one colour, think about combining two colours for a mottled effect.

- Avoid putting too many beads with sharp pokey bits at the ends of a necklace that rest on the back of the neck. Likewise, don't use spiralling half knots at the back of the neck, because they also make wearing the necklace uncomfortable.

- Always take into consideration the weight of the beads and buttons in each project. If a jewellery piece is too heavy, it won't be worn.

- Get a full-spectrum light for your work area.

- Learn to play with the materials with no forethought of a finished piece of jewellery; just play with combining knots and see what you come up with.

- You cannot singe the ends of silk or cotton cord and expect them to melt – singeing only works for nylon cord.

Index